Once Upon A Time in Colombia

A Novel

Benjamin Fisher

Inspired by true events. . .

"It has been my experience that folks who have no vices have very few virtues."

-Abraham Lincoln

Introduction

Airports. I always found myself in airports. Whether it was to pick her up, her up, or her up, or adding to my collection of stamps in my worn, beat up passport; only a year into its life. I somehow always found myself in airports.

I dropped out of college only a couple months before graduating to pursue my dream, or when I had been living under my parents roof, my distraction—women.

My whole life I'd only been good at two things, although their relationship is quite obvious—and complimentary: bullshitting, and getting women naked. Millions of people use their talents to launch successful careers. So, why couldn't I? I left college to be a pornographer.

Let me start by telling you a little bit about myself. My name is Benjamin Fisher. Fisher used to be a name that stood for something. It was a name and family people trusted and respected. My father, the Princeton MBA, and my mother, a successful movie director, had never envisioned their accomplishments. Unfortunately, I had always found a way to bring this name—and its respective bank accounts—down.

My first trip to South America marked the end of that era, and the beginning of a new life, and happiness for me.

It's hard to say exactly where my new career path came from. I guess I could say it started six years ago when I first had the pleasure of exploring the opposite sex. After which, women became a life-long passion—an addiction. Six years after I lost my virginity, I chased women as if my life depended on it. I lost friends for sleeping with their girlfriends. I lost girlfriends for sleeping with their friends. I thought of only one thing—women.

If there is one thing for sure about my family—whether today, 6 years ago when I had my first sexual encounter, or 24 years ago before I'd been born—whatever we decide to do, we do well. I remember telling myself those lines as I got off the airplane in Bogota for a two-hour layover on my way to my final destination of Medellin, Colombia. Sitting in the airport waiting hall, I took out a yellow pad of paper and began writing about my trip. I gave up after a few scribbles about always being in airports. I vowed to keep writing during my trip, and if I was successful, one day I would turn it into a book. My writer aspirations were choked by another side of me, the Fisher side. I thought to myself, "one day if you're successful . . . if?" I recited my motto for my family, "Whatever we do, we do it well, and I am the best at what I do."

A woman on a loudspeaker announced last boarding call. Next stop Medellin.

Chapter One

I bought a cell phone at the Jose Maria Cordova International Airport and hailed a cab to take me to the Black Sheep Hostel in El Poblado, a ritzy part of town where I was going to be staying until our studios were ready for the girls. After checking in and settling into my private room I took out my address book and looked up one of the three phone numbers I had in Colombia. The first two numbers were for friends I had known for more than a decade, already situated down there. I dialed the last number first, that of Ruben Hernandez, the first manager I would hire, and my future business partner.

Now, I'd never met Ruben, but he'd been recommended to me through Alejandro and Estaban, my business partners back home in Miami. I had my doubts about giving so much responsibility to a stranger, but they had insisted.

Fifteen minutes after I called Ruben he was at the hostel. One look at the guy and I could understand why my partners had recommended him so highly. He was 6'4" and 240 pounds of pure muscle with long, dark hair. He was the epitome of a womanizer. Before I said a word to Ruben, I knew this would be the beginning of a long and successful partnership.

We'd never seen each other before, but for some reason, people like us can sniff each other out. We met eyes among the throng of backpackers standing between us. He smirked. I smirked. We shook hands without saying a word, and left the Black Sheep Hostel, getting into his Mercedes.

Ruben spoke only limited English, and when he didn't want to hear what I was saying his understanding of my Spanish would become selective. Even though he didn't speak perfect English, his Mercedes blasted Cypress Hill, and when I opened the door smoke poured out of the car. It felt like home. As the Colombian weed got us higher, the Mercedes took us higher into the mountains surrounding the city. The sun began to set as I took my last hit. I stared at her below us. She was like nothing I'd ever seen. Medellin looked like the product of an orgy between Bangkok, Mexico City, and Miami.

Riding through the slums in that Mercedes made me feel like a king. Ruben yelled at people on the sidewalk for no apparent reason. He didn't do it to show off; he just didn't give a fuck about anything. He wasn't scared of anyone. The inhabitants of the slums looked at him the way I did, with a look of shock. It was 11:00 at night when the weed began to make my eyes heavy. Ruben insisted we drink Aguerdiente, the official drink of Colombia. I declined, but promised him we would the next day. He took me back to the Black Sheep where I slept and dreamt of the adventure that lay ahead of me.

Ruben picked me up at 10:00 the next morning. I opened the door to get in the car. In broken English, Ruben told me, "Today we go fishing."

However, between Ruben and I, fishing was a misnomer. Fishing was more like throwing dynamite in a barrel. Our goal was 20 girls working around the clock on live webcam chats, and we had less than a month to do it. We were working as an affiliate studio for one of the most popular adult webcam sites based out of the United States. At this time, it was already a billion dollar industry. A quality girl could net us $1,500 a week. That's a lot of cash...

Ruben and I drove around Medellin for about two hours, getting slapped in the face by about every girl the guy had ever slept with—which meant a serious beating. We decided to hit the sex shops, and see what possibilities talking to a few people in the various stores would open up. After 15 minutes, we arrived in Zona Rosa. The neighborhood was unique in only one facet; a number of years ago some government officials thought they could stem prostitution by forcing it to one area. Prostitutes and criminals moved openly on the streets, causing the families and businesses there to move out—those who could afford to move out. The others were forced to stay and adapt in order to survive. Warehouses became brothels and hotels. Retail shops became sex shops, boys became girls, and guys like me became rich men. Ruben opened the car door for me.

The three girls working the shop could have all been on the cover of a magazine had they been born in New York or Los Angeles instead of Medellin. Nevertheless, they had been born in Colombia, so they wound up working at a sex shop. I began talking with the first girl.

"I need help finding some items."

"Sure, what are you looking for?" She said, smiling.

"I need a couple of things. Costumes, nurse's outfits, maid's outfits, dildos."

The Blonde behind the counter raised an eyebrow. "Having yourself a party?"

"What's your name?" I asked, moving closer to her.

"Veronica."

"Veronica, you wanna make some real money?"

"What do I have to do?"

We have a winner! I told Veronica about the job. I explained to her that she'd be making 450,000 pesos a week, about $185 American. She couldn't believe it—I love Colombia!

By now, her two co-workers had overheard our conversation and were curious. They walked over to introduce themselves to me. Four hours later, the three girls had quit their jobs, and were lying naked in my hostel bedroom posing as Ruben and I photographed them.

My confidence changed that day. I had always been a player. I always knew I could pick up girls, but for the first time in my life, I felt like I could do anything. I was never the same after that. I never treated people the same. I developed a swagger in my walk, and went from just another college kid to something more, something better— or worse, according to some. After that night, I never had to visit another sex shop to recruit girls. I would approach policewomen, girls at funerals, even girls coming out of church services—I shit you not.

I knew where I was going, and for the first time in my life, what I would accomplish. I knew no obstacle would stop me from getting there. I knew I was destined to become a pornographer, and I knew I was about to become very rich.

Chapter Two

Ruben told me he had a girl who his friend had talked into working for us about a month earlier. Her name was Erica, and she worked at another webcam studio in Medellin, but Ruben's friend had convinced her to quit that job. The only issue was that Ruben and his friend had been a little too ambitious and convinced Erica to leave her job three weeks before I arrived in Colombia, before the studio had even opened. Erica was getting impatient and was threatening to return to her former employer.

I was tired and it was late. Ruben and I had already gotten our first girls, and I didn't see the rush. I felt on top of the world—a high from my progress, the weed, and the women I'd been meeting.

I was ready to smoke one last joint, and call it a night, but Ruben kept insisting. Because Ruben's selective understanding of my Spanish was currently off, and he was already driving us to meet the girl, I decided I didn't have much of a choice. Fuck it. This is what I was here for anyways. I had nothing to lose besides a little sleep and alone time—and everything to gain. I decided to roll with it. We drove south to Envigado, a Medellin neighborhood known for being the hometown of some of Colombia's most notorious drug lords. This was Ruben and Erica's neighborhood. Ruben parked the Mercedes and told me they will be there soon.

"They?" I asked.

Ruben explained she was coming with his friend who was fucking her; the one who convinced her to quit her job. We sat inside the Mercedes waiting. Ruben popped in a Shyne CD. The song *Bad Boyz* vibrated through the car, and Ruben bounced from side to side while lighting a Swisher Sweet blunt. After a few hits, he passed it to me. Erica and Ruben's friend was running late. By the time they arrived we were half way through the Shyne album and two and a half Swisher Sweet blunts had been consumed. I began to doze off when Ruben woke me to tell me they were around the corner. We got out of the car. I looked around and saw the only two people on the street, and they were walking toward us. The girl was wearing a tight black leather jacket, blue jeans, and black heels. The guy, Ruben's friend, looked more like he belonged on the cover of the Shyne album we were just listening to than anybody I had yet to see in Colombia. They walked over and Ruben introduced me to Andres and Erica. Andres broke out in a strong outer borough New York City accent, "You Estaban's boy?"

His English surprised me, but the weed made me too lazy to ask questions. "I'm Estaban's partner."

"Estaban's one of my homeboys."

Erica interrupted the pleasantries. She immediately wanted to know what was going on. She was pissed! She had quit her job and only recently found out we didn't have a studio, equipment, girls—we had almost nothing, and she felt screwed. She told me that she hadn't had work for three weeks, and she was getting frustrated. She wanted to know when she was going to start. I tried to respond, but the Swishers and the long day made my Spanish incomprehensible. Andres translated for me. "We have had some delays. I apologize for this. I know this has been a hard time, and you took a lot of risk jumping ship and coming to work for us, and this will not be forgotten. I am here to make sure you are working by the end of the week. To tide you over until then, I have 250,000 pesos for you."

I handed her the money and she smiled for the first time since I'd met her. She was tiny, hovering around five feet tall, but her body was compact, solid, and most importantly, desirable. She wore her black hair in a ponytail. She had tan skin, but with the makeup she had on, and with the contrast to her hair, her skin looked as white as a Geisha. She had braces, and I wondered if they would turn off potential clients. I shrugged it off. They went well with her petite body. I soon realized I found her braces and small body sexually enticing. Maybe it was the marijuana, but this woman who was so elated and gracious for my cash advance of about $100, was giving me a hard on. Andres translated for me to Erica, that we would be in contact soon. I had him tell her to enjoy herself for a couple days. "Quit worrying, have a little vacation, see whoever you want to see now, because starting Monday, you won't have much free time."

She smiled and thanked Andres and myself, then gave me a warm hug and a kiss on the cheek before walking off. The three of us stared at her ass as she went, appreciating every stitch of her jeans. I waited until she was out of my sight to return my attention back to Andres.

"Man, you guys owe me for this one. Wait 'til you see her naked dude, this chick is bangin'."

"Yeah, she's good looking man," I said, nodding, "If she works out I won't forget it. I'll hook you up with some cash later on."

"Good with me. I can get plenty more bitches too if you want. Just ask Ruben here." Andres translated what he'd said so Ruben could understand.

Ruben nodded his head, smiling. "Si, si, esta bien."

The three of us got in the car and lit the third Swisher Sweet, the one we had been smoking when I dozed off prior to meeting Andres and Erica. Shyne came back on. Andres was jamming in the backseat, singing along, shoving Ruben in the driver's seat as he bounced side-to-side.

"So what's the plan for tonight?"

"I'm going to sleep man, we had a long day." I said.

"What? Nah, no way my dude! I got some more bitches to introduce to you."

Andres gave directions to Ruben in Spanish. I told Ruben to take me back to the Black Sheep, but his selective Spanish seemed to not be working again. Instead of my hostel, we arrived at Parque Lleras, a hotspot for the affluent locals and tourists comprised of bars, boutique hotels, and as its name suggests, a park. Andres and I got out of the car and opened a bottle of Aguerdiente that was in the trunk. Ruben moved to the passenger seat and rolled another Swisher Sweet.

Andres took a swig of the bottle. "You from Miami?"

"Yeah. Where you from?"

Andres pointed to his traditional homeboy Yankees cap. "New York baby, born and raised in Jamaica, Queens, but my parents are from Medellin, and my grandmother still lives down here. I used to come back every summer when I was a kid, Ruben lives on the same block as my grandmother, and we've hung out since we were little."

Andres and I got to know each other. The Aguerdiente helped with the process. He told me he'd been a street racer in New York, and that *that* was his passion in life, until he'd gotten his driver's license revoked for street racing. That's when he had started, "Colombian Dreaming," mimicking the Beach Boys *California Dreaming*. In Medellin, everything was cheaper, girls are cuter, and most of his family was down there already. He'd been living in Medellin for a year by the time we first met.

At first, he'd been driving taxis, and hustling pot. But, six months before I'd met him, he had gotten a job as an English teacher at an adult education center. His experience as an English teacher would end up being a great tool for our business, helping our employees develop their relationships with international clients.

Ruben finished rolling the Swisher Sweet blunt, and got out of the car to join us. He lit it up, and switched between the blunt, his cigarette, and the bottle of Aguerdiente. I almost got sick watching him switch back and forth between the three. He passed the blunt to Andres, who took a few hits, and passed it to me. I took a drag and held it. I saw stars and different colors enter my vision, even as I closed my eyes. I stumbled, causing both Ruben and Andres to laugh. I passed the blunt to Ruben.

Andres grabbed me playfully around the shoulder, "Welcome to Medellin, my nigga! We don't play around here!" A saying I would soon find out was one of Andres's favorites, that he would often repeat whenever he completed a difficult task, or pleased me in some sort of way. I tried to get a hold of myself, think serious for a second. I didn't want to look too fucked up in front of these two.

I asked, "So what the fuck are we doing out here?"

Andres told me we were waiting for some girls he knew. I took another swig of Aguerdiente, and the burn woke me up a little. I was able to stay focused until the girls arrived. The girls wound up being two sisters, the eldest of the two being all of 17. Of course, I didn't know that yet.

Lina and Silvia were both good looking, but Lina was much more attractive than her sister. Lina had dyed blonde hair, with a hint of her natural black showing; hazel eyes, cream skin, and her Colombian curves. Her sister, on the other hand, was darker. I always found dark girls attractive, but she wasn't well put together. While Lina had on a tight white blouse that emphasized her chest, Silvia was wearing a large gray sweater, which didn't leave anything to interest us. I was disappointed to see that Ruben was already involved with Lina.

We drove to a club called Circus. Inside the club, I bought us two bottles of Buchanan's Whiskey. It cost the equivalent of $150. With this flash of money—almost half the minimum wage for a month's work in Colombia—I could see Lina's attention shifting from Ruben to me.

Underneath the table, our legs began to touch. She asked me what my name was, and I told her, "Ben."

"Ven." A play on my name; Ben, insinuating *cum, or, "Ven aqui." Come here.*

Lina and her sister laughed.

"Yo estoy veniendo," *I am cumming*, I said. I looked over at Ruben to see if I had crossed a line, but he didn't seem to mind. In fact, after a few drinks, he told Lina to switch places with Andres and sit next to me. By this point, I was rubbing my hand on Lina's inner thigh as she rubbed her leg against mine. I excused myself to go to the bathroom and asked Ruben to come with me. Andres joined us. In the privacy of the bathroom, I asked Ruben if he was okay with me hitting on Lina. Ruben and Andres both looked at each other and laughed it off.

Andres quoted a Snoop Dogg song, "*It aint no fun, if the homeys can't have none!*"

We returned to the girls and continued drinking. I turned to Lina, who was looking in my direction. I grabbed her hand and began to kiss her. She kissed me back. The whole table stopped their drunken laughter, and went silent for the performance. When we were done, we turned to our audience, embarrassed, and laughed it off. Andres made some noise, slamming his hand on the table and yelling out, before throwing chips at us. We all laughed. I grabbed Lina and took her to the dance floor, where I did my best attempt at a Meringue. After we finished, the club's lights went on and they announced they were closing for the night. We went back to the Mercedes stumbling over one another in our drunken state. Lina had her arms wrapped around my waist, and her head dug into my chest. I asked Ruben, Andres, and the girls who was going where. Ruben said he was dropping me off first, because they all lived in the same direction. In my drunken Spanish, I asked Lina if she wanted to come back with me. She agreed, so I told Andres, who translated the new plans to Ruben.

Ruben dropped Lina and I off at the Black Sheep around 4:30 in the morning. I opened the front door. While the street outside had been dead quiet, the hostel was full of travelers lying around drinking beer and watching movies. They watched as I walked in with Lina. The receptionist called me over and told me I couldn't have guests. After I told her I had a private room she reluctantly let us enter. We made our way through the room of curious faces and I unlocked my door. Lina took a seat on the bed, and I opposite her. I took out some weed and began to roll a joint. We smoked while I played some tunes on my laptop. My bed was cluttered with various work related documents, apartment listings that we would turn into work studios for the girls, budgets, and calculators. I threw everything on the floor and gently grabbed Lina, moving her to the bed. I kissed and began to undress her. She didn't speak while I was taking off her clothes. The submissive way she looked up at me turned me on even more intensely. After I had her in her unmentionables, I began to undress myself. She got up from her position under me and helped take off my shirt, kissing my stomach and lower abdomen in the process.

I moved to the side of the bed and took my jeans off. Lina slipped her hand over the bulge in my boxers, reached up and slowly pulled them down until I was able to kick them off. She bent down, kissing just below my abs, making her way to the base of my penis, where she flirtatiously slid the tip of her tongue.

She glanced up at me, a smile on her lips, before closing her eyes and fully engulfing me in her mouth. She slid down as far as she could, then slowly back up, flicking her tongue against the tip. I fell back over the side of the bed in pleasure, trying to return the favor, but it felt so good, and I couldn't move myself into position, so I slid my fingers inside her instead.

With me still in her mouth, she began to moan. I knew I wouldn't last long if she continued so I pulled myself from her mouth. I could feel the hard throbbing, as I wanted more. She knew it and let out another moan of excitement.

I softly moved her onto her back, spreading her legs, and sliding the thin fabric of her thong to the side as I pressed my mouth between her legs. As she wrapped her legs around my head, I couldn't take it any longer.

I pushed myself up, and pulled away from her to grab a condom, knocking anything left standing in my way onto the floor, but I couldn't find one.

I looked at her, disappointed in myself for not being prepared for this situation, but I saw she was looking back at me. Her eyes were large and dark as she beckoned to me with her finger. She slid her hand between her legs, inviting me. I moved toward her, and as I did, she kissed my stomach. She grabbed my shaft and began to stroke it. She leaned back, moving me to the entrance between her legs. I slid in, enough to penetrate and lubricate myself, and then pulled out. She raised her hips, beckoning me to go deeper, and I did. My third slow thrust went as deep as I could. I could feel her insides readjusting to accommodate me, then the back of her cervix, as I began rhythmically moving in and out of her. She slid her legs around my lower back pulling me into her as I moved out.

We went from slow movements to hard thrusts. She dug her teeth into my shoulder. I could feel the pressure at the base of my shaft begin to pump. I knew I'd cum soon, but I didn't know if I could pull out-I didn't know if I wanted to pull out at that point. I wanted to cum in her so bad. I looked at her, "Yo puedo venir?" *Can I come?*

Lina let out a loud moan, "Si! Si!" she screamed.

I didn't know if she was screaming yes in pleasure or accepting my request, I was not even sure if she had heard my request. It was too late. Fuck it, I hope for the best and thrust harder.

"Dale!" She whispered, *Do it!*

Chapter Three

I woke up to my alarm, a throbbing headache, or both. I'm not sure. I threw the alarm clock on the floor. It stopped making noise but my head didn't stop hurting. I looked at the empty space next to me and saw a note scrawled on the pillow. It said "555-756-4232 *Lina, llama me xoxo.*" I laid the note on the pillow and rolled back over. I put my hands over my eyes to stop the light that was penetrating through the closed shudders. *What the fuck did I do last night?* I thought to myself.

After a few minutes, I got myself together enough to walk to the bathroom. I looked at myself in the mirror, thought back to the night before, and threw up. I managed to get most of it in the toilet. I held onto the shower door to prevent myself from falling over and slowly climbed into the shower. I turned the water on and sank to my knees, unable to move—a mix of exhaustion, alcohol, and disappointment with myself over my reckless behavior of the night before. Twenty minutes later I dragged myself up from the bathroom floor, turned the shower off, dried myself, and dressed. I left my room and went to the kitchen, where a complimentary buffet was waiting. After coffee, orange juice, salad, bread, and eggs, I started to feel a little less like death. I used the bathroom again, splashed water on my face, and took two Tylenol. I looked in the mirror, and told myself that I wouldn't let my stupidity from the night before affect my job and everything we still had to do. People were depending on me. In the middle of my pep talk my phone rang, it was Andres. He told me

Ruben had gone home with Silvia and sent Andres to fill in for him, assuming that would be okay with me.

My head still hurt, but the question allowed me to forget about unprotected sex and focus on something else. *Almost any subject was more comforting.* I thought about the situation for a moment. Andres had made a good impression on me the night before. I decided I wouldn't mind seeing his view of the city. I told him it was okay, but asked about his job at the English school. He said I didn't have to worry about it since he still had sick days that he needed to take. Besides, he wanted to see what Ruben and I had been up to. He said he'd be at the hostel in a half hour. So, I found a chair until Andres showed up. Every minute I sat there, I waited for one of the male backpackers sipping their coffee to ask me about who I was with the night before, but nobody did.

Finally, somebody did say something to me, but it wasn't one of the travelers from the night before. The receptionist, a cute Colombian girl named Diana, told me somebody was waiting for me in the front.

I put my dishes away and made my way to the front. Andres' body took up the entire width of the entrance. He's a big guy to begin with, but between his presence, and a puffed up hip-hop inspired bubble jacket (I soon found out concealed a pistol) he seemed much larger than his actual size.

"My nigga," he said, and slapped me five. "You aight this morning?" He laughed. "You tear that pussy up last night?" He poked at me playfully.

"I don't wanna talk about it."

His comment reminded me of my hedonistic pursuits. Under my jacket, I felt the pinch of the blood test I knew I would have to take for my lack of responsibility with Lina.

Andres looked around. "So where's Lina at?"

"I don't know. When I woke up she was gone."

"Man, let's get out of here and look for some bitches we can actually get on camera without getting in trouble."

We walked to the car, and Andres lit up a Kools cigarette.

"What do you mean get in trouble?"

He took a drag of his cigarette and looked at me, smiling. "Dude that chick just turned 16!" He put on his sunglasses, "Welcome to Medellin my Nigga! I told you we don't play in this motha fucka." The Mercedes burned rubber for about ten seconds before we actually left part of our tires, along with Andres' wicked laughter behind us.

I was quiet for a few minutes.

Andres' laughter died down, and every few seconds he turned to sneak a glance at me. He must have realized that I didn't share his sense of humor on the subject of sex with underage girls. He tried to chisel away at the silence.

"Oh bro, don't worry; it's not like that in Colombia man. Don't worry about nothin."

27

"In the future, please tell me if a girl is underage."

He nodded his head and muttered, "Aight, aight, you got it Papa." He looked at me, "What are you thinkin?"

"It's dark in these sunglasses." I looked at Andres through my Ray Bans. With his deep Colombian tan, he seemed more like a shadow than a man sitting next to me.

"Aright, then we're good." I said, smiling.

I liked Andres almost immediately. He wasn't the type of guy I would have hung out with back home in the States, but at least there was some familiarity and shared cultural connection. He had spent a lot of time in Miami and knew it well, but I guess more than anything, it was nice to have someone to speak English with.

Chapter Four

By now, I was well acquainted with the city of Medellin and its inhabitants. I had my favorite restaurants, and was staying in a hostel run by a German man, a few years older than myself who had bought a beautiful Spanish Colonial mansion in El Poblado and turned it into the Pitstop Hostel—a favorite for young backpackers travelling through Colombia on their respective pursuit of adventure. My private hostel room was coincidentally called, "The Pussy Pink."

Above the sign was another and this one read: NO DRUGS PLEASE. We all had a good laugh at this while conducting various films and interviews there. It was in the confines of those four walls, first room on the right on the second floor of the main house where some of the best days of my life happened. One of these days was spent filming single-mother Maria.

Maria was in her late 30's, and you could see it on her face and her skin. What she lacked in those areas, she made up for with her body. As she opened her legs and peeled her flower apart for the camera, Andres and I turned our heads sideways to peer in. We then looked at one another.

"Dude, we have the best job in the world." Andres said.

"How did she fit three kids through there?" I asked.

We did have it good. We were young, surrounded by women, and we were rich—at least compared to 98% of the local population. But, our luck wasn't all-good. By the time we'd rented a second room at the hostel the owner was catching on to our game and wanted us out by the coming weekend. We needed a studio and we needed one fast.

When I first came to Colombia, if someone had asked me what I would have a more difficult problem with: renting locations, or getting girls. I would have definitely said getting the girls. Getting the girls in Colombia was easy, just smile, try to make a good impression, and look trustworthy enough to let you in. Getting in their apartments on the other hand, is a different story.

The different story. . .

"In Colombia, nobody trusts anybody." Ruben first made that statement to me as we drove away from the third landlord that had rejected us that day.

As we drove away, I asked Ruben why it was so hard to rent properties in Colombia. He smiled, but didn't say anything. Three kilometers down the road, he pulled over to the side of the highway.

"Come here, I want to show you something," he told me in his thick Paisa accent.

He got out of the car, and I followed his lead. He climbed across the four-foot highway railing into a thick of trees. He pulled the vines apart and motioned for me to follow. After about four meters of fighting our way through the thick brush, we made our way to the edge of a ravine, looking out over a wide rocky stream called Las Palmitas.

Ruben told me that in the late 80's he would come to the river with his friends and they would wait to see the dead bodies float by. He told me as a child he never had to wait more than a half hour to see one. Escobar, in his later years, had developed so much paranoia that he quelled it by killing those closest to him. This and other bodies of water floated away Escobar's fears.

I suddenly realized that I was a foreigner in a dangerous business, in a place that within my lifetime, was considered the most violent city on the planet. I wondered how long we would have to stand there today to see a body float by. My feelings of fear and excitement didn't last long, as Ruben who was on the phone with another landlord interrupted my thoughts. We had an appointment in a half hour in Envigado. We fought our way back through the brush and climbed into our cave of marijuana smoke and Shyne records. We cruised to Envigado.

We were ten minutes late for our appointment, but it didn't matter since nobody in Colombia seemed to keep track of time. The landlord, a middle-aged balding man of European descent, showed us around. We lucked out. The place was huge! Almost 279 square meters and the price was right, only 2,100,000 pesos a month, or $875 My mind went into over-load as I tried to do the math of how many girls I could fit into each room. I told the landlord that I wanted the place, but I guess I looked too eager, because he began to question me.

"What exactly is your business?" He asked, seeming somewhat skeptical.

I told him, "Webcams. Girls chatting on the computer."

He was quiet for a minute. "Do you have a Mercantile Registry?"

"Of course," I responded, "It will be ready before we begin work."

He thought it over for some time before shaking his head. "I'm sorry but I don't think I can rent to you."

"Why not?" I wanted to yell, but managed to hold my cool.

"There are other businesses and respectable people who work in this building. It's just not the sort of business I support or feel comfortable renting to. And I think the other neighbors in the building would complain about hookers coming in and out all the time. Think about how you would feel sharing the elevator with some of these girls if you were coming to do business here. Think of what impression it would give their clients. I'm very sorry."

He had a good point. I hadn't thought about it from that perspective. Don't get me wrong, I love my employees, but nobody is going to mistake two webcam girls for accountants.

I thanked him for his time and we left. We drove away, but I couldn't get the studio out of my head. I kept seeing it with the beds ready, the computers, and curtains. I saw my dream in front of me, and this landlord just snatched it! We drove in silence the entire way back to the Pitstop. Ruben sensed either that I was deep in thought, or was having the same visions I was. When we stopped outside the hostel I shook his hand and pulled him close,

"Do whatever you need to do, to get me that last place."

I stumbled out of the car. Tired, and disappointed, I somehow made it to my room and fell asleep. I dreamt of my non-existent Envigado studio and the girls hard at work. I saw myself in the studio. I was staring at a brunette from behind, wearing a red bra with matching panties, who was playing with her hair and teasing somebody somewhere in the world over the webcam in front of her. She turned to look at me, but she wasn't Colombian, or one of my workers.

It was Amanda, my girlfriend

Chapter Five

The dream, and my phone ringing, jerked me awake.

My first thought was that my girlfriend was calling me. I felt a sense of guilt as I thought back to Lina—unprotected sex, and underage flesh. I calmed myself before answering.

It wasn't my girlfriend; it was the landlord from the last place we'd seen the day before.

"Don Fisher?" He said, adding the entitlement to my name. "Don Fisher, I am so sorry for the confusion we had about renting our space. After thinking it over I decided it would be my pleasure to rent you the office I showed you."

I put the phone down. I didn't know what to think. Had I still been dreaming? What had happened? After I got out of bed and brushed my teeth, I called Ruben and Andres. A half hour later, they were outside the Pitstop on Ruben's motorbike. They knocked on the door and entered the room.

"I just got a call from the landlord we met yesterday."

They glanced at each other.

"Yeah, what did he say?"

"He said the studio is ours. What did you guys say to him?"

Andres and Ruben looked at each other with grins on their faces.

"Don't worry about it man."

"Seriously, what the fuck did you guys do? How did you get him to give us the studio?"

The two of them started laughing. "Don't worry about it man! Let's roll a joint and check out our new place!"

"We're not going anywhere 'til I know what the fuck you guys did."

They looked at each other and Ruben nodded his head to Andres.

"Well, we went to go and see him like you asked us to, and he was being all stubborn and shit. So I pulled my piece on him, stuck it to the back of his head, and made him sign the contract."

"You did what? Are you fucking crazy?"

Andres had the look of an innocent child on his face that didn't realize he had misheard the teacher's directions.

"But. . . But you told us to do whatever we had to do to get the studio?"

"But yeah. . . I meant. . . "

I stammered as Andres and Ruben looked at me to finish my sentence. They didn't understand how they messed up. I realized they were my soldiers; they would do whatever I told them to do. When you're the boss, watch what you say. Especially, when you're in Colombia and your employees believe in you.

Chapter Six

Now I admit, I didn't necessarily agree with my managers' tactics, but they were effective and I was very happy with the results. Any anger I'd had with the two of them dissipated the second I opened the door to our new studio. Andres suggested rolling a joint, but a new adrenaline filled me—we had work to do.

The next stage wouldn't be exciting, but it did need to be done. We had to get high-speed internet, wire the studio for twenty or so computers, and buy said computers, modems, keyboards, and furniture. Those were just the items we planned spending time and money dealing with. You wouldn't believe how many cleaning supplies are needed for a business like this.

I slowed myself down and reported to Alejandro and Estaban. When I told them the story of how Ruben and Andres negotiated the terms of our lease, they were less surprised than I'd been. I guess they hired our managers for more than just their boyish charm. This was the way of Medellin. Holding the phone with one hand, behind the window's glass I looked down at the street below. A woman was yelling at a man, she could have been a prostitute. Maybe she wasn't, maybe he was a lover, or maybe a brother. Maybe I didn't care. I stopped thinking about it. I had seen it too often here. There are only so many families living on the side of the road you can give a dollar to, or you will be there soon yourself.

We took the Mercedes down to El Centro, the downtown of Medellin. Once bustling with hotels and beautiful office towers, it had been a hub for business from every corner of the world, but during years of depression, the neighborhood had been flooded with peasants who had come from the mountains to escape the drug wars. They often wound up homeless, and crime began to rise. The area eventually turned into one of the most dangerous in Medellin. Businesses and their employees moved to the suburbs, and the few businesses that now existed in the area were mostly industrial.

What we were looking for in El Centro was furniture. After taking measurements of the rooms we realized there was no way we could possibly fit enough girls into the studio using traditional beds, so we found ourselves looking for something smaller, such as a loveseat or futon. In El Centro, we found everything we needed. After bargaining with different merchants, we finally agreed to purchase five loveseats. We took three in red, with black pillows, and two in white, with red pillows. They were to be delivered in three days to the studio.

The next task was getting computers that would be fast enough for the bandwidth of the girl's performances. This sounds like an easy task, but in Colombia, things were not always as they seemed. At the time, internet was just becoming widespread in Colombia. Most people knew how to use computers and had email, but went down to the local internet café to use the computer. High-speed internet was extremely hard and expensive to get there at the time. The internet providers were inundated with requests and could take up to three months to deal with an issue or complete an installation.

You see, Colombia had no income tax up to a certain level. The government made their money on what they deemed luxury purchases. A car could easily cost three times what it would in America. Computers were another item that was considered a luxury good. This delicate balance between poverty and luxury helped our business flourish. The high price of "luxury purchases" such as computers and high-speed internet forced girls to come to us. At this point, the only reason we could convince girls to work for the wages we were then paying them was that they didn't have the money to purchase computers and high-speed internet themselves. Nor, the privacy to do such a job from home, but the high price did cause a lot of strain on our budgeting. Alejandro and I calculated the cost of towers, flat screens, webcams, wireless keyboards, and other electronics we needed. We determined that it made more sense for him to buy the towers in the States and ship them to Medellin. The other items would be bought in Colombia.

We had a location to shoot, computers, internet, and beds, but we still needed more girls. We decided to start with three girls working 5:00 p.m. EST to 6:00 a.m. EST, the most profitable hours of the day.

It's hard enough to manage twenty employees. It is even harder to manage twenty lower class Colombian girls working in closed quarters, with very little privacy, doing what we do. Not to mention, every one of those twenty employees had at least a few days a month they were unable to work due to menstrual cycles–unless the client was into that sort of thing, which there *is* a niche market for.

This was just one of the many complexities of the webcam business that we were beginning to learn. I finally got some time to myself. For the next two days I retired to my old room, *The Pussy Pink,* where I was, "welcome as long as I was on hiatus from work," as the owner told me. I had two days to relax before we began broadcasting. I was worn out mentally from work, and I was worn out physically from trying to keep up with Andres and Ruben's partying. I could have stayed at the studio for the two days and sent Andres and Ruben home, but I wanted something away from all of that for just a day or two.

Chapter Seven

I spent the next day by the pool getting shitty at the bar watching some European tourist girls play in the water with the hostel owners Labrador Retriever. I smoked joints, contemplated our operation and all the people I had met. I wondered if my life was possibly in danger, and thought about Andres and Ruben pulling the gun on the owner of the property I was now using as my base. My thoughts were interrupted by one of the European girls, who turned out to be German.

"Do you mind if I have hit of your joint?" She asked.

"You're blocking my sun." I replied. She moved to the side. "What's your name?"

"Heidi."

"Nice to meet you, I'm Ben." I passed her the joint. "Do you want to sit?"

"No, thank you. I go back to swim with my friends." She handed the joint back to me. As she walked away, she looked back and said, "Nice to meet you Ben."

I looked at the time and saw it was already six o'clock. D-Money, a friend of mine from back in Miami, was supposed to pick me up to go salsa dancing at Mangos that night.

I went up to my room and masturbated to photos we shot of one of the girls from the week before. I showered and got dressed. When I arrived downstairs to meet D-Money, I saw the German woman who had interrupted my joint smoking session sitting alone at the computer. She saw me and smiled.

"Hi Ben!"

"Hi. What are you up to?"

"I wait for friend." She looked over to D-Money, so I introduced him.

"This is my friend Daniel. We grew up together in Miami, he lives here in Medellin, and tonight he's taking me out."

"Where are you guys going?"

Daniel spoke up. "A couple of clubs in Itaguai, why don't you bring your friend and come with us?"

Heidi looked at me.

I nodded my approval. "Yeah, why not?"

Heidi was smiling to the point of laughter, "Okay!" she said.

We waited for her friend, and got drinks by the pool bar. They played Bob Marley, and I felt good. I started to eye Heidi. She was older than my original impression of her at the pool, most likely in her early 40's, but she wore it well. By now she'd gone up and changed into a red dress, revealing, yet still classy, allowing me to peek just far enough up her leg to leave room for the imagination, and boy, was I imagining. We had a couple more drinks and my hand was beginning to feel up her back. She looked over and smiled. We called a cab and headed to Mangos. Outside the club we bought a bottle of Aguerdiente, drank, and said hi to some friends who worked as street vendors there. She was intrigued by how many of the locals I knew. By eleven o'clock, we arrived at Mango's, to our disappointment, we were one of the only groups there. Then again, it was Tuesday in Medellin's winter. Only the DJ's girlfriend was dancing, after a few shots of whiskey I grabbed Heidi and began to salsa dance with her. D-Money must have been feeling a little drunk because he was cracking a smile for the first time of the night since seeing Heidi's girlfriend. Heidi's friend, Bertha turned out to be 300 pounds. We had another drink and D-Money even danced with Bertha, twirling her and laughing. We left around three o'clock, and I had my arm around Heidi's waist, occasionally moving down to palm her ass. She whispered in my ear, "Why do you want me?" I whispered back, licked her ear, and told her how sexy I thought she was.

"But I'm too old for you; I'm old enough to be your mother." She responded.

"Yeah! But, only in Colombia," I said, and she laughed understanding my joke on the sexuality of Colombian women.

When we got back to the hostel, D-Money wished me and the two girls' goodnight. We shot the shit outside; everybody knew what was going to happen. The ugly friend eventually said goodbye to Heidi and we went upstairs to the *Pussy Pink* to explore, the pussy pink.

Next was buying outfits and toys for the girls. My partners and I debated about whether to buy everybody the same toys and outfits for a cheaper price in the United States or to buy everything for the girls based on what they wanted—for a much steeper price in Colombia.

Eventually, we began supplying designer underwear and other products from the United States to our employees, as well as a Christmas calendar with different products they could purchase outside of our industry. Even though we made money off these items, I would like to mention that we still sold it for cheaper to these people than anybody else could in Colombia. For example, an Iphone in Colombia could cost $500 and up. We could bring two with us on the plane. If one of us was there every couple of weeks, that would usually pay for the airplane tickets.

While organizing the internet, refrigerators, building cubicles, and buying sex toys, we had to think about how we were going to manage twenty employees. I had never worked for anyone but myself up until that point. I didn't know what to think, I thought I knew—but I didn't know shit. When I mentioned having girls work sixty-hour weeks, Andres spoke up, "Ben, I know you're Jewish, but damn you're going to kill all our employees before they can make us any money. This is a physical business."

Eventually, a schedule was worked out. When we moved forward and started filling other rooms, and then other studios, we first fit the other American time slots, and then went overseas to fit other places into our schedule such as Germany, Israel, England, and Australia.

After we had targeted the most active hours, we had to figure out which girls would be working which shift. We had gotten over a dozen girls approved for the website, but after so much time had passed, who was actually still interested? How many girls had backed out?

Chapter Eight

The first day only one of the girls we had hired showed up, the first girl who agreed to work for us—Erica. She had worked in the business before and Andres had kept her interested for a long time before we even stepped foot in Colombia. She was an excellent employee. If every girl worked as hard as Erica did, we would have made $500,000 in six months, easy.

Erica believed in what we did. She was motivated. This was the number one problem we found with other employees early on. The girls had no interest in whether we succeeded or failed. They didn't see themselves growing with us or becoming part of our team, they were being used, and didn't care if we were around in six months. The girls would satisfy a short-term debt, save up some cash, and then be on their way, hoping nobody would ever find out. So the question was, "How do we retain our employees?"

We would find girls and they would start and quit a few weeks later, so we developed an incentive plan we hoped would reduce employee turnover. Signing incentives were paid in draws, 25% up front, and the rest in installments over the course of a year. We found two reasons that led to our high employee turnover rate. The first was that girls would come for two weeks to one month, make a good paycheck or two, and pay off a credit card bill and leave. The second concern with turnover was if the girls found a new sugar daddy. After a couple weeks of working for us, these girls could make some good money, start buying nicer clothes, and looking like eye candy again. They were already beautiful; some of them just needed a little cleaning up.

We were a month in and already breaking even. Erica was our Michael Jordan, our leading scorer. She spoke more English, and most importantly, had a higher conversion rate than the other two girls working the same shift combined. We weren't making money, but we also weren't losing money, impressive for any new business after one month. We didn't think so, but in our attempts to examine every little detail, we missed something that should have been blatantly obvious—training. Our first girl was our superstar, of course, we had stolen her from one of our competitors, and she had been in the business for years. Our other employees, however, were brand new to the business, and if Erica didn't like the girl, they were working against each other. If Erica did like the girl, she would train her, but then again, a fight with one would become a fight with both. It became clear that our current arrangement was not working. We began to envision Erica's role in the company being bigger than just working with clients on the web cam. She was smart and she would often share new scenarios and ideas with me. Alejandro, Estaban, and I discussed giving Erica the role of head trainer. We also began to work on our own interactive training DVD. Unfortunately, Erica abruptly quit a few months later, leaving our company, as well as a girlfriend she met while working with us. Word was she caught herself an extremely rich boyfriend, things like that happened all too often in this business.

Chapter Nine

Sex should be able to sell itself, but sometimes sex can't, or at least needed help. We implemented a training program, using some of our favorite personal porn material as examples. Everything was translated into a Spanish DVD, which would eventually be played for all of our employees. The instructional video would greatly reduce the amount of time needed to supervise a new employee. Training included how to prolong each interaction with a client to maximize the amount of time they spent in private sessions; things such as slowing the process of taking off their clothes and working with props.

All these things count when looking to increase profits. Men react impulsively, and a girl who doesn't meet the level the customer is expecting will have a viewer click back quicker than a customer can walk out of a strip club, or adult movie theater. In the end, all those seconds add up to minutes, which add up to dollars.

We taught our girls the appreciation of smiling. I explained to them that they should be enjoying what they're doing, giving pleasure to lonely, desperate people all around the world. But, if they didn't feel that way, they needed to put on a smile as if they did. Nobody wants to have sex with an unwilling partner, well, most sane people don't. I remembered how I felt when I would watch porn. I wanted the girls to look like they were enjoying it, to remember that women like sex as much as men do, if not more, to remember that I was the man in things, to tell the girl where to sit, what to do. I remembered that a girl having sex without so much as a smile or moan was something I would click away from. I could have sex with plenty of girls who would look distracted or bored like that in real life! Why do I need to pay to watch them? I tried to remember what it was like all those times for the past dozen or so years I had been that customer I was targeting, what kept me watching, and it worked out great...

The training video was a miracle. Like sex, alcohol, and writing, I didn't understand how I had lived up until that point without it, and I knew I couldn't live without it in the future. The video was shown over the course of two days, combined with live practice observed by Andres, Erika, or myself. We also taught English lessons at different times. It wasn't hard, we just helped them recognize words they needed to remember; I'll leave *those words* up to your own imagination.

We made sure to treat the girls well or at least better off than they had ever been treated before, during training. We wanted them to feel like they were living, and could live, the high life, as if they'd just won the lottery. For dinner, we would book reservations at a fancy restaurant, reserve a limo, and let the girls take off early after they completed their training.

We had reasons for spending so much money on the girls and doing this. The first was that I was also rewarding myself. There is nothing like going out to dinner in a limo with three gorgeous, *morally flexible*, women. I restrained myself from sleeping with any of the girls that night. The pleasure and reward I felt in that situation was something new to me. It was better than the pleasures and rewards of sex with any girl I'd ever been with. It was my first taste of power...

Secondly, I was trying to get these girls to be dependent on me, dependent to a lifestyle they could not otherwise afford. I attempted to build a second life for them that they wanted to be a part of, something there to keep them when the money has come, the credit card has been paid, the baby has been fed, or a new boyfriend has been found.

During dinner, I pressed them on their feelings about working for our company, what they knew about the industry, about our competitors, how comfortable they felt under the camera, really just trying to pick their brains. A lot of them had very insightful comments. They brought up scenarios that I had yet to think about. Andres sat with us with a yellow pad we always carried in a black leather case, writing down anything that I told him to, and any interesting questions the girls had or that he had. Some girls asked about friends coming to work for us. *What about working with partners?* How would we split the money for these sessions if one employee were paid more per minute than the other? *What if a customer only wants to see a lesbian scene for ten minutes?* Can someone who is free in the next room just walk over and do the work with other girls? I was unable to answer many of their questions. Until then it hadn't mattered to me how they were making the cash, just that they were making it. All I could do was thank them for their input, and assure them I would have answers to their very reasonable questions before they began their scheduled work rotations in two days. The invincibility I had been feeling was weighted by the lock of my jaw—my physical response to the realization that I still had a lot of work ahead of me. Andres met my stare. I knew he was thinking similar thoughts. He gazed back to the yellow legal pad, scribbled something down, and looked at his watch and then back at me.

I took the notes from Andres, and left him with the girls. I smiled at them, making sure to look into each of their eyes, acknowledging that I cared and had enjoyed their company, and told them I was going to start working on answering their questions.

Everyone seemed sad to see me leave, especially the staff of the restaurant.

I gave Andres enough money to cover the bill and tip. The limousine had already been arranged. I was careful about how much I gave Andres in front of the girls. I wanted it to be enough, where they felt that being around me would help them out, but I didn't want them to see too much and wonder why they were only seeing bits and pieces in return.

Joanna, one of our new additions offered to go back with me. I declined while biting my lip and looking her up and down, finally locking eyes with her. "Another night," I told her, "another night."

I caught a taxi and got back to the studio. I needed some weed, and a Xanax–something to relax me. As I had come further and further along on this journey I had begun to booze harder, and take a lot more Xanax. If some sort of math needed to be done, then a different cocktail of drugs would ensue. I suffered from both dyslexia and ADD. I was abusing the prescription drugs and knew they were starting to kill me. I found myself feeling physically weak, but money, Colombia, gangsters, and women will excite you enough not to notice things like death I took a swig of the Jack Daniels sitting at the table and swallowed it with a Xanax. I looked over the notes.

I was tired. Xanax defeated me. I slept with my face on top of the yellow pad, the questions written on it absorbed through my skin, into my brain and my dreams.

In the end, it took me a full day of playing telephone tag with my lawyer in Colombia, and the other one in the United States, as well as the representative of the website we were an affiliate of, about some of the final questions that we needed to answer before going live with our two newest employees. By the time the girls showed up, they had the answers they needed to begin work.

And work they did! We had all of our girls on the East Coast night shift. It's tough working at night, but our girls were enjoying it and word spread fast to the girls in our neighborhood about the possibility to live and party like the rich.

Soon, the need for active recruiting was over, we developed a waiting list of girls interested in working for us. I was thinking about moving from our original three girls to five for our late shift. The dinner I had taken the trainees and Erica to earlier in the week made me wonder if driving past the slums in the limousines was a better form of targeted advertising than a newspaper in Medellin.

After all, I thought, not all of our employees can read, but they sure could understand their friends' new clothes, and see them with half of their body out the sunroof of a limousine.

Deciding on the next two girls was a lot more complicated than it sounds. I kept reminding myself of the troubles I had just a couple of weeks ago with Erica and her allies and enemies. I realized that even though we had the opportunity to recruit our next two girls through our current employees, it might not be our wisest decision. Can you imagine when you have one employee walk in late and threaten to dock her pay for it? The other girls would stand up for her, we would threaten their pay too, and all of a sudden, half of our employees are threatening to quit simultaneously. It was obvious we needed to bring in new people and from different advertising than our own employees word of mouth.

I spoke on the phone about it with my two partners in Miami and we jointly decided that it was worth spending the money to put an advertisement in the local Medellin paper to avoid building further alliances within our employees.

The advertisements were well worth it. The one-week quarter-page ad brought a lot of attention from a variety of sources. We also didn't want too many girls from the same neighborhood talking about the studio, and telling a guy in the neighborhood about the twenty computers we had. We didn't need him and his buddies trying to rob our place. We also didn't want a bunch of angry ex-boyfriends, who turn out all to be homeboys, as our enemies either. They can all be dealt with, but it is a pain in the ass, and a distraction from what you should be doing—making money. Also, looking for someone through print advertisement increased the chances that they were somewhat educated, less problems with English, possibly, less chance of her being involved with a bad crowd, which kept us out of a bad crowd, and most importantly—a chance that she had a passport.

Finding employees who had passports was difficult and the affiliate website we were working for, didn't accept any other documentation from foreign citizens. A solution to the passport issue would save us two days of a girl reconsidering and reneging on her offer, the money on the passport, wasted two days, and possibly rejected other applicants. We started going with our employees to get their passports. If they could not afford it themselves, they could give us something as collateral until they had worked off the debt. After dealing with the passports long enough it became clear there was a bigger issue at play, it was sovereignty. Yeah, we could get around the passport issue this time. However, the real issue was, even down here in Colombia, with your boys pulling guns on people who disagreed with you, limos and Mercedes, naked women, you still had a boss. You weren't free. Somebody else was making the real cash off your hard work, and a thousand other little guys just like you. I began to ask myself, why am I not him? Why am I not the boss?

We went through the regular process of meeting the prospects. We would usually meet them for lunch, explain to them the details of the business, and see if we all felt comfortable with one another. If all parties were interested, we would then go back to the studio and have them undress, take their photos to get approved by our affiliate parent company, copy their id's, and arrange to get them a passport if they did not have one. Here are a few of the stories we encountered while trying to find our next two girls.

Meet Yessica

Yessica was a friend of Andres, actually a former student of his at the English school. The two had stayed in touch. When we first had lunch and I met her, I understood why Andres stayed in touch with her. She had the type of hips that made Colombian women famous. Unfortunately, her style did not match her body. Yessica was shy. We went through the usual motions, she asked about the specifics of the job. She asked if she would have to be with other girls and I responded that it was her choice what she wanted to do. I could see how hesitant she was acting. She asked me if what she did in the performance could be recorded by the people watching. I explained to her no, that *that* would defeat the purpose of the business, so the website has very strict encoding to make sure that wouldn't happen. The lunch lasted for over an hour. Among her concerns was the potential of her family seeing, her boyfriend finding out and leaving her, and just plain fear. She explained to me that she already had a job as an office manager. She was studying for her MBA. She was not our typical prospective employee. She explained to me that she was afraid of not doing well, and leaving her job. After about forty minutes, I got tired of the conversation and simply told her, "So don't do it."

After noticing my patience running thin, Yessica agreed to come back to the studio to take some photos. I had never seen somebody so beautiful with so little confidence. She said that first we would see if she was even approved for the site. I felt sorry for her and began to wonder what her life had been like that could lead somebody so beautiful to such a poor self-image. I pictured regular beatings, and her mother's boyfriends, sneaking into her room late at night. When we got back to the studio, Yessica went into the bathroom to change out of her clothes; it took her a few minutes, like all her actions of the day. When I was beginning to worry about her and what she was doing in the bathroom for so long, she finally came out. It was worth the wait. She held her arms over her C-cup Leonisa bra, a high-class local brand I recognized. I knew she had bought it especially for this occasion, the quality of her bra and matching panties seemed to contradict the caramel beauty they hid. Her hair was black and flowed down to her apple shaped behind. She had dark eyes, and the lighter creamy skin of Costeñas, *the people of the coast.* Andres and I stood silently, and she froze. She asked us if everything was okay. We realized that she had taken our surprise and shock the wrong way, and thought we were looking at her disapprovingly. We snapped out of our trance, and reassured her that everything was great. She leaned against the door, and asked, "So what do I do?" I instructed her to relax, and told her that she looked beautiful. Yessica turned her head away from me, and moved her hair, avoiding eye contact with either one of us. I repeated to her that she looked great, and she had nothing to worry about, that she should be proud of how she looks. I told her not to worry about anything, that if she wanted the job, I was sure she could get it.

"But, you are going to have to learn to relax, and be comfortable around us, around the other girls, and most importantly around our customers," Yessica nodded her head, and moved her hands away from her chest, letting them dangle lazily on her sides.

"So what do I do now?" She asked again.

"Now, we take some photos! Can you pose for me?"

Yessica attempted to pose, and put her hands on her hips, attempting to smile.

By this time, my thoughts were beginning to wonder what I had tried to ignore before. I wondered if this was the right girl for the job.

Yessica eventually felt comfortable enough to make a couple of semi-sexy poses. She turned around for one, revealing an ass you could balance a champagne glass on, but unfortunately, I realized that while the still photos would be enough to get her approved because of her looks, her attitude and shyness would never be able to sell on webcams. Maybe she would get lucky and find a pervert or two who would love a girl who looked like she was forced into doing the job. Her discomfort was unsettling, and I didn't want it to affect the synergy of the others in the studio. I stopped shooting and thanked her for her time, and gave her $100. She was confused, and asked me if she had done something wrong. Andres also did not comprehend the situation; he'd been trying to see this girl, *sin ropas,* without clothes for years, and didn't understand why I was stopping this seemingly act of God.

"Listen, you are absolutely gorgeous. I would even love to take you out, make you my girl here in Colombia if you didn't have a boyfriend, but it's obvious to me that you are not completely comfortable with this job, and the most important thing I'm looking for isn't a girl's beauty, it's her attitude. Unfortunately, or fortunately, depending on how you look at it, you just don't have it. There's nothing wrong with that, this job isn't for everyone."

Yessica slumped down on the bed, feeling dejected. She looked up at me, tears in her eyes. "I know. I just thought I could force myself to do it, the money is so good."

"I know the money is good. Listen, I'm here in Colombia, the money is good being a coke smuggler, but that doesn't mean I'm about to do that. It's not for me. Everybody has their limits, and you'll find your way in something else I'm sure. You have a job most girls in our business dream of having."

She sobbed and nodded her head in agreement, flashing a smile. I handed her a tissue and her clothes. She smiled up at me from the love seat and took the clothes, gathered her energy, and walked to the bathroom.

Andres came over to me, distressed. He whispered, "Dude, what the fuck? She's perfect! You know how many guys will want to see her?"

I had to fight my desires. I knew Andres, for the first time since I'd met him, had let his emotions take over his sense of rationale.

"I know you like her around here naked, and I know you want to see her around naked, but you're letting your testosterone get the best of you, this is not the right girl for the job."

"Aright, maybe you're right, maybe you're not. Maybe she'll get comfortable in front of the camera in a couple of days; maybe she'll wind up doing better than Erica."

"And maybe she won't, maybe we'll have to spend all our time watching her, and the other girls will get off track, or become infected with her depressed attitude, and we'll lose all our customers, and have to close down this little dream of ours. If we had twenty girls working already and had some cash saved up, by all means, I would love to see this girl walking around here naked all day. But we don't, and we can't risk it."

Andres was silent

"Don't ever question my judgment again." I told him.

He nodded.

Melena

Now Melena was no comparison to the beauty of Yessica, but rarely in our first few months of operations would I see a girl comparable to Yessica. However, since our customers never knew of the existence of our first option for our fourth employee, Melena proved to be a highly valuable commodity. Our interview with Melena started as routine as anything in this business can be.

We met at El Exito in El Poblado. (El Exito is like the Wal-Mart of Colombia.) We exchanged text messages until we finally found one another, and grabbed a coffee.

The first thing I noticed about Melena was her personality, she was warm and inviting, a smile was omnipresent, and it went well with her rich green eyes. She joked and talked a lot, about her life, asking me about myself. After a half hour, Andres rejoined us after finding some items we needed for the studio. I asked her if she had any further questions, she said no, and asked, "What's next?"

"Let's go take some photos!"

"Dale."

We took the Mercedes and drove back to the studio. When we got upstairs, I gave her a quick tour around the place. None of the girls were at work yet, and the place seemed dead to me without the hum of computers, the clinking of keyboards, and the hymns of passion that usually filled the rooms. But Melena was impressed.

"We film in here?" She asked.

"Yeah we can film in here." I replied.

I turned on the lights and began to open the shades to let in some natural light as well.

When I turned around Melena was half-undressed. She was standing in a bra, and jeans, her G-String already surfacing as she struggled to get out of her pants. I watched her with one hand still on the window. She looked up at me. After a few moments, she asked me to come over and help her. I submitted. I moved closer to her. She looked me in the eyes and I was close enough to taste her strawberry flavored breath, but I didn't move towards her lips. I moved around her, putting my cheek next to hers and first unbuttoning her bra. I pulled away from her and removed it, looking at her breasts. I felt myself becoming excited. I put my hands on her breasts and inspected them.

I pulled my hands off, "Not bad."

I then knelt down and began to work on her jeans. With her wiggling back and forth, we managed to pull them off together. For a moment or two longer than needed, she stayed a few inches away from my face; I stared directly at her crotch, which had the tiniest patch of moisture darkening the white underwear, illuminating the lips behind it.

I looked up at her, still on my knees, and she looked down at me. Finally, Andres interrupted, "Ben?"

I snapped out of it, and got off my knees.

Andres smiled nervously, he didn't want to piss me off, but he didn't want this to happen either.

"Come on man, we got work to do, let's film this girl, and move on to the next one. We got mad work to do today."

We filmed Melena. She was everything a customer could ask for: responsive to our requests, horny, fun personality, smiled, laughed, the type of girl that can develop a relationship with a customer. A customer who might reserve an hour or two a night, just to sit and laugh with her, pleasure themselves two or three times in between, and just talk about their shitty day with. During the recession that was taking place in America at the time, many men lost wives, and girlfriends. It was a good time for us to be expanding our business.

During the photo session, Melena caught me staring just a little too hard at her to be considered professional. "You like what you see Papi?"

"Where do I sign up?" I asked her.

"So why don't you forget about me working for you and make me your girlfriend. You marry me and take me with you to Miami?"

"Why can't we get married and have you work for me here?"

Melena continued to move around, flexing into different poses. "Come on Papi, you don't want your wife working in a place like this. I should be home cooking for you."

"But, I want a wife that I have something in common with. I mean, what would we talk about around the dinner table if you weren't working with me?"

Melena called me "*un enreador*." It was a word I had never heard before, but would soon become very familiar with. It would stick with me throughout my time in Colombia. Andres explained to me that *un enreador* was a slick talker; someone who could sell ice to an Eskimo is how he put it. It would later become the name of our company—Enreador Studios.

We finished the photos and walked Melena out. Andres and I walked out onto the street below. He called to Melena, "Padonde vas?"

"A la farmacia."

"Por que? A comprar condoms para tu y Ben?"

Melena stopped and looked me up and down, mimicking my impression of her in the studio.

"Con el, nunca usaria proteccion." *With him, I would never use protection.*

Andres and I went to eat. We looked over the schedules, under slot #4 I wrote in Melena. One down, one to go.

Slot #5

Four hours, hundreds of photos a dozen videos, six breasts, three vaginas, and three stories later, we had found our fifth girl. Her name was Paula, she was 23 and had tried working as a prepago, (A prepaid hooker that you order over the phone with a credit card), but had decided it wasn't for her. It wasn't a moral thing; she was just a smart girl, trying to get off the streets and into a safer working environment, away from sexually transmitted diseases, gang rape, robbery, murder, etc.

Although her ID agreed with her claim that she was 23, I couldn't believe it. Physically, she could easily be 23, but she was more sophisticated in the way she dressed, more professional—at least when it came to Colombia. She wore charcoal grey dress pants, a white dress shirt that revealed the top of her milky Antioquian breasts, and a blue scarf around her neck covered partially by her straight hair. She could have easily been one of the beautiful housewife's that married in, and out, of the elite of Medellin, or one of the many female small business owners here that had recently appeared since the end of the drug wars. Whatever the first impression of her, it was clear that she gave off the presence of a confident woman that knew what she wanted, and was going for it. I liked that about her, although I didn't trust it. It has been my experience that people like this are often uncompromising, and unable to seek mutually beneficial solutions when problems arise. They can't distinguish between their dreams, and what reality will make you compromise to achieve such dreams. I recognized these things in her before I spoke a word to her. Through her body language, as well as her clothing. But like her, I was beginning to not to be able to differentiate between my dreams and what reality would make me compromise to achieve them. Reality asked for more time, to wait for someone else, someone more amicable to instruction, but my dream was too close to let things like reality get in my way.

Chapter Ten

Melena began training the next morning. Paula started the day after that, giving both of them sufficient supervision during the training process, as well as allowing Melena to have her first shift alone with Erica, for support and instruction, while Paula finished her training.

Training went according to plan, and three days after meeting Paula for the first time, she had disposed of her professional attire and traded it in for blue lace panties, a bra, and garter belt. Melena was everything we had hoped for, and Paula was everything that my senses so desperately had tried to alert me to, and I had tried so hard to ignore. Melena was open to instruction, often staying after her shift was over to review footage with myself, or Erica, determining what she did wrong, and why a customer left a private chat. We had set up our own closed circuit televisions in the rooms to better supervise the employees.

Melena was quickly becoming our second starlet. If this worried Erica, she was able to conceal it very convincingly. In fact, Erica and Melena began to spend their breaks together, and a few weeks later, started to come into work together. There were a lot of whispers in the studio that the two had become more than just friends—A point that was confirmed a few weeks later, when the two asked if they could work their sessions as a team.

Thanks to Erica's tutelage, Melena was not only averaging our second highest length of time in private chat, but she was building a large fan club as well. The fan club gave members access to letters from the model, as well as pre-recorded videos and photos not available to non-members. This added another dimension to the job for both management and the girls. We had to either split the twelve-hour shifts to include time for photo shoots and videos, or make the girls work even longer hours. What percentage of fan club memberships would an employee receive? At the time with just a few employees, it had been easy enough. Erica had hours worth of footage from her old studio, as well as personal footage shot by her or whatever girl (or boy) was lucky enough to wind up with her at the time. I handled the letters and updates—offering them in both Spanish and English. I had to figure out what to write for the girls—what they did that week, sexual fantasies, all sorts of things. Even for a writer, it can be a difficult task, especially when trying to handle it in a studio. Once I had created five new stories, I had to change the English to sound poor enough so customers would be convinced it was actually the girls writing. After getting the girl's approval of the content I would write for them, it had to be uploaded to the website, where after receiving approval from the website, would finally be posted. When you are doing weekly updates for five girls, the photos, video shoots, and writing, can become quite strenuous. We needed to get more organized. If we were struggling with five girls, how would we be able to handle twenty?

But, fan club membership would have to wait; another problem had to be dealt with. . .

Our first four girls were working well, but Paula was not. She came to work on time, and stayed until the end of her shift. But that's about all she did. She wore the outfits, and spent most of her time chatting. But chatting did not make us money. She would need to do more to continue to work with us. Showing up was simply not enough.

But what was enough? Was someone who did half as much work as Melena enough? Paula wasn't trying to manipulate us by just getting by. I understood her point of view—when she was in private chat, she did what the customer requested. She also stayed after hours to shoot extra photos and videos for the few customers who had signed up for her fan club. But, it's hard to know what is not considered good performance when you haven't defined it.

Eventually we decided we needed a new payment structure. With just five employees, I could micromanage Paula and tell her that she needed to *do this* or *do that* differently, or that she was spending too little time in a private chat. But, we wouldn't be able to do this when we had more girls to manage.

We decided, like almost all sales jobs, to switch our payment system to a performance-based one. All employees would receive a base salary. Then, based on how much time they spent in private chat, as well as at what price, plus the number of members in their fan club, we would determine their pay.

On top of this, we started a new incentive program offering cash rewards, or paid days off, for the highest earners of the month in private chats and fan club membership. The biggest prize was a week's pay for the overall breadwinner of private chat and fan club membership. After a few weeks, Paula had left our studio. We left on amicable terms, and had agreed that if the need for some sort of still photo shoot came up, I would get in contact with her.

We were way behind schedule. None of the management had said anything—like I said before; in Colombia, it felt like nobody has a sense of time. But in Miami, they sure did, and my partners had seen all the photos, heard the stories, seen the checks, and were hungry for more–and so was I. But being on the ground there, I was a little more realistic then my partners back in Miami. I knew how much of a battle it was to get even this far, but, I had two partners back home, and there was only one of me in Colombia. The decision was made: all systems go to filling the remaining slots available on the night shift.

There was another factor that motivated my partners, which I had yet to discover. Colombia is a predominately-Catholic country, and Christmas is a very big deal. We needed to move fast for two reasons: the girls were desperately looking for jobs to be able to, either go on vacation during Christmas, or to be able to buy gifts for their loved ones. Second, the entire country of Colombia pretty much shuts down for the month of December and parties for a month.

If we were going to get into a schedule, and train employees, we would need to start now, or wait until after Christmas. There was no way I was waiting any longer. I didn't quit college to come back with a couple of hundred bucks. I didn't leave my girlfriend and my family for this. I needed this, and I needed it to happen quickly.

I split up our team. Andres would handle recruiting to fill the remaining slots. I would remain at the studio during the night shifts, making sure employees were on time, working well, and all the other issues that come up with management. Ruben, with his Mercedes, would handle both resupplying whatever was needed in the studio to keep us running, as well as picking up all the items needed to accommodate future employees we expected to hire.

I coordinated with my partners in Miami to have all supplies for our computers shipped directly to the studio. Ruben handled researching flat screen monitors, and other computer accessories. He had to find the most affordable yet reliable monitors, keyboards etc., and negotiate with the store owners for a cheaper price on the items for buying in volume. Ruben would then repeat the same process back in El Centro at the shop where we purchased the first five love seats. Ruben was also responsible for building the shelves to hold the monitors, and building the cubicles to give the girl's privacy.

Within seven business days, we were fully stocked with computers, love seats, and working areas, but we still didn't have all the girls. Not yet at least…

Andres had been working hard, finding more girls who would be interested, but for many of them, the time slot did not work. Many of the girls wanted to work a day shift to be able to hide what they were really doing from boyfriends, husbands, children, for these cases, Andres happily took their photos and information anyway, and I submitted them to the website for approval. We knew that if we kept working hard, the time would soon come when we would shift our attention to focusing on the day shift. But, for now, we still needed to fill the night shift.

The next week was a hectic one. When all the workstations were set up, we brought in four new girls for training. Both Erica and Melena had to take time off from their usual clients to train the new girls. With the purchase and international delivery of new computers, another month of rent, the love seats, I was becoming anxious. If these girls didn't work out, and Christmas came, we would be out of business. My mind tortured me with "what if's?" What if we fail? What if I have to return to Miami? I was no longer in school, I would have to move back in with my parents, and get some minimum wage job. The thought scared me to death. How could I go from this, to bagging groceries? In the movie *Fight Club*, Edward Norton says that after *Fight Club,* the volume of everything else in your life is turned down. That is exactly how I felt about Andres and Ruben, the girls, the studio, and Colombia. I couldn't go back to do something else. For me, there was nothing else. . .

My fears were gradually assuaged. Hard work, Xanax, time, and a lot of naked women helped me bury these thoughts deep inside. Every night, a new girl showed up for training, and every night Melena or Erica would have to disappoint a lonely customer somewhere in the world by taking time off to help the trainees.

With the new arrivals, I knew I had to change something. I couldn't have my two best saleswomen losing loyal clients because they had to supervise the new employees. With Ruben's job complete, I left him to handle managing the girls already working, and after a week we were able to relieve Melena and Erica of their training duties, so they could focus on their clients. I was exhausted; I had been inside the studio almost 24 hours a day for over a week. My skin was pale, and I needed some fresh air. I was losing my mind. I wanted a vacation, to return just for a day or two to the mansion hostel in El Poblado, to the *Pussy Pink*. I just wanted to sit out by the pool for an entire day, and not look at a schedule or a bill. But, this wasn't the time for that, so I did the next best thing—I split up the training with Andres. He would train girls half of the nights, and I would handle half of the recruiting. Ruben was left in charge of the photos and videos for the fan club, while I remained in charge of the fan club letters.

Here are a few stories of some of the girls that wound up filling the night shift for us.

Angela

I wish I could describe Angela for you, but the truth is, by this point, the faces around me began to blur. I am not sure if that was from the sea of caramel colored skin and black laced panties that were constantly filling our studio, or the Xanax I had become heavily dependent on. Whatever it was, the girls, at this point, began to lose their faces. What I do remember about the first meeting with Angela is something she said.

After getting through the usual description of the job and what it entails—hours and salary, Angela agreed that she wanted the job. I pulled out the yellow pad that Andres had used to cover any thought that popped into my head, and began to look over the monthly schedule. I asked her:

"When do you get your period?"

"I have a problem. I am not able to have children. I rarely have my period, maybe once or twice a year."

"That's great!"

Angela and I both laugh at my comment. Then I had registered what I had just said, and what I was becoming. I felt something inside my stomach drop. Outside we were laughing; inside I died just the tiniest bit.

Carolina

Carolina was a friend of Angela's. In the beginning, I had tried to avoid hiring friends of employees, but we had to make some exceptions. I was, again, letting my dreams create my reality. But, Carolina played the part of model well, she posed like a girl on the cover of Maxim. The rich boyfriends she kept on the side had paid off for her; her *Besame* underwear and expensive make up made me dream that I was somewhere in California working for Playboy in an expensive studio, and not in Medellin.

Now that Angela was working, we were able to skip the usual meeting at El Exito, Carolina knew exactly what she was getting into, and she began training her first day after taking her preliminary shots needed to get approval from the website. After awhile I was beginning to forget about the fear of failure that had taken over me just a few weeks before. I started to think that we could still do this. Carolina was number twenty. We had filled the East Coast night shift! But, I wasn't able to continue thinking about the subject. Carolina broke my train of thought, and spoke to me in a tone that I could tell was a precursor to bad news.

"Ben, before I work for you, there is something that you need to know about me."

My mind was rushing, *what could possibly be going on? Is her boyfriend a serious Mafioso and she was sent undercover, and now is asking for a bribe, or even worse, asking us to shut down?* As you can see, I was desperately in need of a vacation and another Xanax. But her request turned out to be much more benign then I had thought.

"I can't do anything anally, you see I have hemorrhoids. Is this a problem? Do you want me to bring a doctor's note?"

I slumped my shoulders forward, falling into the chair behind me, and smirked. I looked at her and the opened window revealing the green of the Medellin mountains behind her lingerie-clad body.

"No, I don't need a doctor's note. But, clients will ask for anal, and you will lose some clients. Explain to them that you can't. Andres or I will teach you how to type that in English. It just means you're going to have to work extra hard to try to make it up in other ways for those clients."

Carolina looked relieved. She walked over to my side of the desk, and used one of her legs to spin my chair to face her. She climbed on top of me, put her arms around my neck, looked me in the eye, and kissed me.

"Thank you." She said.

She got up and walked out to begin her first training session with Andres. I stood up and reached for the bottle of Jack Daniels on top of the bookshelf—my first session with the whiskey for the day.

Chapter Eleven

We had finally reached our goal of twenty girls working the East Coast night shift. While we knew that in this business, commitment and consistency were things you couldn't count on, we were ready to shift our priorities to expanding our business beyond the one shift.

All of our girls working the East Coast night shift we're making us a hefty profit. Everyone seemed happy, and every week, a new battle would ensue to see who would win the three different prizes. We had worked out the fan club responsibilities as well, dividing the writing between Andres, and my partners back in Miami, and myself. I was even able to get some rest. I took a few days off in my old room, the *Pussy Pink*, at the Pit Stop Hostel. I enjoyed the last of my Colombian weed, because after this small vacation, I was flying back to Miami.

The trip to Miami was to be a short one. I hadn't seen my parents or my girlfriend in over two months now. My girlfriend and I spoke regularly on the phone, but my parents and I had barely spoken during the trip. They had no idea I had started a porn studio in Medellin. But, there was another more important reason for the trip back to Miami. With the East Coast night shift filled, and making us good money, my partners and I needed to decide what time slot to fill next. One argument was to start with a day shift, working in the same studio, another idea was to rent a second studio and hire more girls to work the same East Coast night shift. Coming up with a resolution that would satisfy both my partners and myself was my real reason for returning to Miami.

Chapter Twelve

Airports. Again, I found myself in an airport. But this time it was Miami International, one of my least favorite.

After staring at my passport for a few moments, and inspecting me, the U.S. Border Control Officer stamped my passport. I walked through customs. I was home.

My first stop was the apartment I had shared with my girlfriend. She was waiting for me in one of the summer dresses that fit her tall physique so well. I put my bags down, and kissed her. I knew she was expecting a sexual reunification. I slid the straps of her sundress off her shoulders, and the dress fell to the floor. I tried to pretend that I hadn't changed, that I was still the same person, that I was still so sure I was in love with her, and that she was the one for me—that there *was* one for me.

I guess months of staring at naked, silicone sculpted bodies can change your perceptions about life and love.

Amanda was lying on the bed; we made love, and then smoked a joint together afterwards. We caught up on little things that lovers speak about in bed, the type of stuff that just doesn't fit into an international phone call. I told her more about Andres, Ruben, and the studio. I told her about how Andres and Ruben had pulled a gun on the landlord for us to get our studio—a detail I was afraid to mention on the phone. I told her about Erica, and Melena. She asked me about the women—if I was attracted to them.

Before I ever thought about running a porn business, especially one in Colombia, I consulted with my girlfriend, whom at the time I believed was my partner, and would one day be my wife. Being as young as we were, she fully supported the idea as long as I kept my hands off the girls, nobody was getting hurt, it was legal, and we were getting paid.

The next stop would be to my parents, whom I doubted would take the news as receptively as Amanda had.

My parents didn't take the news as badly as I had thought they would. My mother didn't really say anything; she grabbed the wooden dining room table for balance, and sat down. Finally, she broke the silence by asking me if there was anybody being harmed, if it was legal. I tried to comfort all her worries, explaining about our licenses, the great pay the girls made, and the privacy (which I overstated to her), how happy the employees were to work there, etc. I told her how Erica and Melena had actually started a relationship after meeting at the studio. She was not impressed. She told me she needed a minute, and waved me off. I left the room and went outside for a cigarette. My father joined me with two glasses of whiskey. He sat by one of the many pieces of garden furniture that could be found in such a large expanse.

"Come join me boy."

"Yes sir." I went to join him. I sat down across from him, and he slid me the whiskey. "Thanks Pop." I told him.

He took a swig, and looked down at his drink.

I knew he was about to speak. "That's Reservoir Straight Rye Whisky you're drinking there son; one of the best."

I took a sip.

"It's very good sir."

"Hmmmh. I know it is very good, I got an entire crate of the stuff in storage here." He took a long pause, and for the first time diverted his attention away from his whiskey and faced me. "You know how I can afford to have an entire case of this shit in my storage facility? How I have a warehouse just for the shit I haven't used yet?"

His voice rose—getting angry.

"Hard work and ethics boy! Did I teach you to be a thief?"

"No sir! But this is—"

He cut me off.

"This isn't stealing? You are stealing son, you just don't see what you're stealing. Pornography is a sickness, cocaine makes a good business, doesn't mean you should get into that!" He says the exact same line I had told Yessica just a few months earlier. "What you're doing is the same as starting a poker website. It is a sickness all the same, and you're stealing the girl's dignity too—their innocence."

I smirked a little and responded, "Somebody got to that innocence a long time before I did, Dad."

"I don't like it one bit. How are you getting paid? I don't want one of these girls to wind up suing you; I have to get you listed as an independent. Shit Ben! What the fuck are you thinking?"

I was silent.

"Is it money? Listen, I know I have been tight with you. I just wanted you to be able to appreciate the value of a hard earned dollar, but we have a lot of money son, you don't need to do this." His voice had changed from fury to pleading. "What about school? How are you going to handle this semester? You're going to handle a full load of courses and run a business in a different country?"

"Well, that's the other thing I wanted to talk to you about."

"Talk to me about what?"

"School."

"What about it?"

"I'm not going, at least not this semester."

My father looked at me, his eyes changed quickly from sorrow back to anger. He forced himself to gulp down his whiskey. I think the spirit was the only thing holding him back from attacking me at that moment.

"Give me a cigarette."

I passed my father a cigarette. He sat down again; this time slouched over, the posture of a defeated man. He didn't look at me, but he did speak to me at least.

"Why are you doing this to us?" He paused, "Did I harm you in anyway? Everything that you wanted, I did my best, really, didn't I?"

I put my hand on his shoulder.

"You're the best man I know Pop. One day I hope to be half the man you are."

"Well, then start by getting out of this Colombia mess and back to school. I didn't complain when you chose some small school in the middle of nowhere over Princeton, but now I refuse to let you ruin your life even further than you already have!"

"I get... I get this rush there Pop. I can't explain it... The city, the people, everything is connected, and just... just so alive. I feel alive there Dad... and I'm good at this Papa, really good at it."

He looked me directly in the eyes; it was hard for me not to gaze into his blue eyes.

"You would have been good at anything you had chosen to do Ben."

I knew I should have given him more of an explanation, tried to make him understand—maybe he could never understand. I had to get out of there; I could already feel my legs beginning to wobble like Jell-O. I touched my father on the shoulder one more time, "I got a plane to catch Pop. I love you. Tell Mother good-bye and that I love her. I will write you soon." I walked towards the fence gate. My father was still sitting, facing away from me, when he called out.

"Ben?"

"Yes sir?"

"Be careful out there."

When I pulled up my rental car to Estaban's house, I found my two partners and some other close friends waiting in the driveway. I parked and exchanged greetings. We spoke for a few minutes, making chitchat, some of us smoked cigarettes, and one of my partners opened a bottle of Don Perignon. We all had a drink, and then, Alejandro, Estaban, and I went in to speak. The others made their way to the backyard to swim and barbeque, and wait to party with us after we made our next move.

The first issue was the time of the next shift. There were arguments for a day slot and to rent, or even buy a second studio and begin the next group of girls on the same shift. It was decided we would rent a second studio and fill that location with the same shift that had been so successful, while simultaneously filling the day shift in our first studio.

Once this was settled, we had to decide on whom the girls were going to be. Thanks to Andres' recruiting, we already had seventeen girls to choose from. (Remembering that some of them will have changed their mind by this point). We looked at photos, and I did my best to remember the girls I interviewed. Andres explained on a conference call about the girls he had seen, levels of English, what type of documents they had, who they knew, etc. It took us the entire day to decide on the first five, and backups for them. In less than 24 hours, I had told my parents I was working in porn in Colombia and dropped out of college, had sex with a woman I was trying to figure out if I was in love with, and possibly made the most important business decision our company was facing in our entire first year. By the same evening, I was having dinner in Medellin. What did you do today?

Chapter Thirteen

A few days after arriving home in Medellin, we received the keys to our second studio. But this time, no guns were needed to get us the contract. The deal was done through the family of one of my partners. Now that we had built a very successful first studio, the two were more willing to use their connections to get us porn studios, hence less faces got broken. I was happy about that, and the guys were all happy about the studio. It was a dream come true, a four bedroom residential in Las Brujas. Most importantly, each room had a bathroom with a shower—which for our business was a gem.

Las Brujas is an upscale suburb of the city—the towers provide breathtaking, panoramic views of the mountains surrounding Medellin and the clouds that hover in above, distorting where the clouds begin and mountains end.

Yolanda and Sandra were trying out for the first positions in our second studio. The two girls were friends from Las Brujas. When they came to the studio, already knowing what they needed to do, they seemed undecided, looking at each other every time I commanded the two to drop their clothes. Their indecisiveness turned me on; my hard on could be evidenced through my mesh *North Carolina Tar He*els basketball shorts. Yolanda had blue eyes, and skin just a little darker then my Gringo skin. Sandra on the other hand was darker, with black hair and brown eyes, and skin as creamy as my morning cappuccino.

After about ten minutes of trying to get the two to undress, I asked them what the problem was. They apologized and told me how much they wanted to do this, but they wanted something to drink before being in front of the camera for the first time. I sent Andres to pick us up a bottle of vodka, as well as all the ingredients needed to make the drink that used to get me laid in college all the time: the Apple Pie.

The drink is easy enough to make, it's just half a shot Smirnoff Vodka, half apple juice, a sprinkle of cinnamon on top of the drink, consume, and then licking whipped cream off of your partners hand. Well at least the first drink was off their hand, if the game went well, then the licking of whipped cream would move onto other body parts. This was luckily the case that night between Yolanda, Sandra, and I.

After Andres returned, we all had a drink, or two, or three. The weather sensed our change of mood and the sun began to poke through the grey winter sky. Yolanda moved from the bed to my laptop on the desk, she played some Reggaeton. We kept drinking and the two girls began to dance, every few drinks, removing another item of clothing, or two. After a few songs, the girls were finally loosening up. We began to shoot the two of them. The photos went well, the clothes were gone, and so were their inhibitions, a little too gone.

Andres and I looked at each other. The Reggaeton continues to play in the background, and the bottle of vodka still held enough liquor to keep the night going. Yolanda must have been having the same thought, because she danced her way over to the vodka bottle and took a long swig. She puts her hand over her mouth, and fell laughingly on to my lap. She kissed my neck and ear. Andres took a photo of the two of us. Now I wasn't quite sure what to do at this point. I had a policy of never sleeping with the girls. Like any other business, this can lead to complications. The girls can start to think their job with the company is safe as long as they're fucking the boss on the side. But, I *had* had a hell of a few weeks, starting on the day shift, and the second studio. I had never even taken a night off to party and celebrate having our first studio running 24 hours a day at maximum capacity. I decide that night would be my celebration…

We continued drinking, and the four of us passed the camera around, taking photos as the night moved forward. I made more Apple Pies for us. The shots, as planned, moved from hands to necks, to breasts, butts, abdomens…. Young people are the same at college in Miami, as they are in a porn studio in Medellin, the same everywhere I guess. The music continued to play and we enjoyed a dance or two from the young ladies. Sandra asked me to make her a mixed drink. I complied, making her a vodka-cranberry. I passed her the drink.

"It's not mixed very well; you might need to stick your finger in to mix it better," I said.

"I never have a problem getting my finger in," she responded.

I looked her up and down, and bit my lower lip. "I hope I won't either."

She laughed and placed her hand on my now naked shoulder.

"Keep giving me drinks and you won't." She looked over at Yolanda. "The same goes with Yolanda too." She looked down towards my crotch, which we both could see was twitching as blood filled the area covered only by my thin shorts.

A few drinks later, I asked Andres to leave the three of us alone. He looked at me pleadingly to let him stay. I again repeated my order to Andres. His shoulders shrugged and told me he would be back at the studio at 9:00 tomorrow morning.

He left me with Yolanda and Sandra.

I moved to shut the lights, but the girls stopped me, and told me to lie down. I did, and they lay down on opposite sides of me. They teased me, forcing me one way to kiss one, then the other licking my ear, or kissing my abs. Yolanda went down on me, and Sandra hovered her "lower lips" over *my* lips.

After a few minutes of attempting to share me, Sandra wrapped her legs around me and began to motion me lower.

Yolanda moved across the room and flipped off the lights. From the window, a light blue of the moonlight left a pale impression over the three of us. I felt myself being lifted, as if I had reached another dimension, not heaven, but somewhere in between here and heaven. The pleasure I felt was too much to exist in this lifetime. Yolanda and

Sandra must have sensed this feeling of pleasure I was experiencing.

After we each had climaxed, the three of us looked at one another, laughed for a minute, and collapsed. We held one another tightly in the bed, eventually falling asleep together. Yolanda got up and put on a sweater and sweatpants to sleep in. Now that my adventure to a different dimension was over, I regained my ability to speak:

"How are you going to sleep in those, it's so hot in here?"

"I'm really cold on the outside, but warm on the inside."

"I can vouch for that."

The Beginning of the End

As a kid, I had always fantasized about being born into a different time. I often imagined what it would have been like to be one of the conquistadors—on top of my horse, no law but the ones I chose to enact, taking whatever women I could catch, robbing whatever resources I could find. These are the thoughts of a 12-year-old boy, confined to the frustrations of puberty, freed by the imagination of escape and an easy solution to all of life's questions. But of course, I wasn't born in the 16th Century, so being the owner of a porn studio in Colombia was about as close as I could get to being a conquistador. I jokingly told my partners that, in a way, we were conquistadors of the age of globalization. We were still robbing foreign lands of their precious resources, and still having sex with as many of the local women as we could. But, the times for fantasies and the easy solutions of childhood would not suffice much longer.

We had been in business for over a year now. I rarely thought about Miami, and had very little communication with anyone there, most importantly, my parents, whom I spoke to maybe half a dozen times since my last trip back to Miami when I told them about dropping out of college and my new profession. I knew losing them was one of the possibilities when I got into this business. When I did speak with my parents it was awkward. I was ashamed of myself. I wasn't necessarily ashamed of the business; I knew my parents thought I could be doing something more lucrative and entrepreneurial than this, that was the shame, as well as the business. I began to despise myself for the awkward position I had forced my relationship with my parents' into. I would call on birthdays, mother's days, and other holidays, but rarely would I catch them. When I would catch them on the phone, they were always in the middle of something, or on their way out. It was never a good time. I obviously knew my parents in their retirement had not become busy overnight, but I swallowed the awkward position I had forced them into, as one of the potential risks of being in that industry.

Ever since realizing what my relationship with my family had become, I knew my dreams of staying in this business for a long time would mean the loss of those relationships, permanently. For a year, the idea had stayed in the back of my mind, I kept telling myself—as others also told me—that my family would get over it eventually.

Amanda, Alejandro, Andres, and my other confidants would all have a similar solution to the issue: money. Once my family had seen that I was making money, and that I was okay without their financial support, my family would come around. For one year, I forced myself to believe this lie.

I told myself it was a loss I was willing to bear, at least temporarily, when the thought crossed my brain, or when I would avoid the urge to pick up the phone and call them.

Andres, Ruben, Medellin—that was my family now. I didn't want to have to choose between the two. I hadn't asked my family for anything, or used the family bank accounts since stepping foot in Colombia. I was no longer a drain on my parents financially. Far from a drain, I was making close to six figures in my first year, which in Colombia went much much further. The entire studio grossed close to $500,000 in that same period. By this time, we had three studios running 24 hours a day. Besides this, we had also begun to film DVD's. I couldn't give up now. We had come so far. These were the thoughts rushing through my ADD brain as I waited at the Medellin Airport to fly back to Miami. The reason for this trip was to discuss one of the only possibilities left for growing our business— building our own website.

As an affiliate studio, we were free from many of the responsibilities that come with having your own website, things such as maintenance costs, and most importantly advertising and liability. However, because the website takes on these risks for you, they also take a large chunk of whatever the girls working in your studio produce, usually around 60%. We had two choices; continue our time proven method of building studios, and continue to work as an affiliate and get less than half the money the customers were paying to see our girls in our studios, or try to build our own website. For weeks, I had sat on Skype with Alejandro and Estaban, as well as website developers, attorneys, and internet marketing consultants about the pros and cons of the two strategies. Each day brought up more questions, more possibilities, but few answers. Ruben and Andres had the managing thing down by now. I was no longer needed to handle the day-to-day operations. By now, both Alejandro and Estaban had quit their full time jobs and were strictly pornographers— often going down to Medellin for a week or two at a time relieving me of some of the pressure and rush I had felt before, then leaving me with nothing but my thoughts and questions. Building a website could be the distraction I needed to keep myself here in Colombia and away from resolving issues with my family. These were my last thoughts as I reached the security checkpoint at Medellin's airport. I looked at the passenger in front of me. The police had opened his suitcase and gone through his luggage piece by piece. I began to go over what I had packed. I panicked just the tiniest bit, picturing the officers finding an empty baggie of reefer that I would often discover in my pockets or strewn around among my other possessions. But luckily, the police found nothing and I boarded my flight and flew "home." As the airplane left the soil of Medellin, my heart dove deep into my stomach. It was the feeling you get before dealing with old, buried problems.

Chapter Fourteen

This was my fourth trip "home," since arriving in Medellin what already felt like a lifetime ago. In a way, it was a lifetime ago. I now felt like a new person, much different than the person I had been in the U.S.A. Usually, I would arrive at Miami Internation Airport to Amanda, go back to our apartment, make love, and then go on to meet with my partners about whatever issue had brought me there, then back to Medellin as quickly as possible. This time I skipped meeting Amanda. The time I had spent away, the money I had made, and the things I had seen, had all taken a toll on our relationship. It was not over yet between the two of us, but I was in no rush to see her. I rented a car, and met Alejandro and Estaban at a strip club near the airport. If all went well, I could take a flight later that night back to Medellin and not even tell anybody else I was there.

I made my way over to the titty bar. There were only a few cars in the massive parking lot. Two of them I recognized as Alejandro's and Estaban's new rides. Both had traded their cars in since the start of our business for foreign luxury cars that they leased for around the same amount that an employee of ours could make in two months.

I walked inside, paid the ten-dollar entrance fee to the black giant working as the security host. I made my way through the mist, the smell of stale beer and broken dreams to find Estaban and Alejandro sitting in a booth in the back with a bottle of champagne and two blonde strippers. When they saw me, they both got up and put their arms around me.

"Welcome home Papi!" said Estaban, grabbing my shoulders to look at me. He patted my growing stomach, "I see you've been enjoying the food of Colombia."

I hugged Alejandro, and we sat down, Estaban introduced me to the girls and we had a glass of champagne. After the glass, Alejandro excused the girls, and asked them to come back later. We all broke out yellow pads, laptops, and calculators.

First, we discussed the possibility of staying as affiliates and filling more studios. The problem was that we would need to hire more managers. Andres and Ruben were great, but they each could still only be in one place at one time.

But, this was just a small issue; all three of us knew what the real one was: we felt like our girls; we were being fucked, the only difference was by whom.

The idea of continuing as an affiliate was dropped, and we began to discuss creating our own website. We went over the costs of building the website: maintenance, search engine optimization to increase our number of views, liability, and the legal ramifications. How much money would we offer to affiliates in the same position we had been in up until now? How would we ever find affiliates at the beginning? Without enough affiliates, how many studios would we need running to build a successful website? What other ways of making money were there for us that we could tap into by having our own website?

Over the course of three hours, we went through the possibilities, doing research about other websites, looking at their traffic flows, making phone calls to e-marketing specialists. We had all taken a couple of speed pills to try to maximize the little bit of time we had to figure everything out. The three of us loved to work under pressure. When the numbers were becoming a little clearer on our Excel sheets, I began to get extremely excited. We finished the champagne and continued working until the place began to crowd for the evening. When it finally got too noisy to concentrate, we paid our bill and made our way outside.

In the parking lot the three of us smoked cigarettes and looked over the numbers, Alejandro had his laptop open on the hood of his BMW. We were not anywhere near finished, but we had some rough estimates. Ultimately, we would need around $200,000.

"So if we're going to do this we need around $200,000. I hope that we won't need to spend all of it, but I don't want to start anything until I know we're going to be able to finish it. We still need money for rent for the three studios we have, which is around $30,000 a year. We're going to have to open three to five more studios to have enough employees working around the clock. We need to pay their salaries, and we need at least $50,000 for SEO work on the website."

We were all silent for a moment before Estaban spoke.

"I don't have that type of money right now."

Alejandro seconded this.

"What do you mean you don't have that type of money right now? What the fuck have you been doing with your money?"

Alejandro said, "I bought two apartments with that money."

"I bought a finca." *A country estate,* said Estaban.

I took out a second cigarette. My hands were shaky and sweaty from the speed and the South Florida climate.

"Okay. Okay. So we take it in baby steps, we begin by setting up the other studios we need to even start building the website."

The guys were silent in their agreement.

"Then we'll see in 3-6 months, and quit fucking spending your money! Start saving up!" I said.

We were all silent for a moment. The idea of waiting another 3-6 months didn't sit well with Alejandro.

"What about your inheritance money?"

I was surprised. I hadn't thought about the money left to me by my grandmother since we had started the Colombia operation.

Alejandro continued, "I mean $200,000 is nothing. You're not speaking to your parents anyway. They're not going to even know about it. Think about it, we do this now, and instead of each making $50 or $60 grand in the next six months, we could be making triple that."

Estaban stepped in, "And as soon as we start turning a profit, Alejandro, and I won't see any of it until that $200,000 is back into the inheritance account."

Alejandro, who knew me better than anybody in the world, knew exactly how to get me interested...

"If we start right now, within ten years, you could easily make a couple million, quit the business, make up with your family, and never have to work another day of your life before your 35th birthday."

He had me…

Both of them leaned against Alejandro's BMW, trying to read me for some sort of response. I tried to mask my interest, and looked at my watch to see what time it was.

"It's late; I'm going to try to get the last flight out tonight. I'll think about it and speak to you in a few days. Either way, one thing is clear; we need to open more studios."

We shook hands and said our goodbyes.

I got in my rental car, closed the door, and waited for the A/C to begin to work. When the car had cooled down to bearable temperatures, I thought about the possibility of using my inheritance money to fund the website. I thought about my mother, Amanda, and my father. I thought about using the money I had made to quit the business and go back to school. Then I thought of Andres and Ruben, and the excitement of Medellin and our business. I was confused. For over a year, I had been confused. The more time I spent in the business I figured the less it would get confusing. However, the opposite was true; things weren't black and white like they teach us as children. This business, and my life, was very much in between the two, I was stuck in the gray, the same gray that often occupied the sky over Medellin where I was also stuck. I witnessed honest people committing crimes, dishonest people engaging in acts of good, and people who both I and themselves didn't know what to define themselves as, doing acts of good and evil, sometimes even at the same time. Every woman I encountered, and every new story I heard, I felt a little more distant from the reality I had known for the past twenty odd years. I laid my head down on the driving wheel for a moment, looked up and let out a deep sigh of relief. I decided I was going to take the money I still had left over from my salary and begin with building the new studios. After that, see how I felt, if things with my family had gotten better as I hoped they would, how things were with Amanda, and of course, with Medellin.

I drove back to the airport, protected from one of the "Sunshine State's" many sudden showers, by the rental car. I returned the car, and took the bus to reenter the departure terminal. I bought my ticket, sat and waited. I thought about the new studios, the new people, and stories I would encounter. In front of me was a TGI Friday's. I had three hours to kill, and the bartender was a blonde, the type I rarely got to see in Medellin, I made my way over and had a Budweiser. I tried to distract myself from the business by staring at the bartender's cleavage. She didn't notice. She was skipping through the channels on the flat screen above the bar. She finally stopped at a channel playing a slasher movie. Two teenagers are making love; they are too distracted to notice the serial killer sneaking up on them. The bartender pressed the information button, a blue line at the bottom of the screen appeared, the movie was one of the first films my mother worked on. It was the last thing I wanted to see right now. I gulped down the rest of the beer and left the Fridays. But the movie stuck in my head, I was in Miami, I could have stayed, and drove two hours to my parents' house and told my mother I was out the business. Maybe with my new experience filming, she could have gotten me work on some new movies coming out. I had my inheritance. Then just as quickly as this line of thinking floated through my mind, a different voice appeared. Fly back, take the money from your inheritance, and build your dreams! In front of me was a Bank of America ATM. I walked to it, and slipped in my family card. I looked at the balance. $200. The speed I had taken made my body spasm. My first thought was that this must have been a mistake. I checked again, and again. I stayed for five minutes, until someone from the line that had formedbehind me finally said something. I pulled myself away from the ATM machine and sat down. I took out my ATM card, and began to dial the number on the back. I spoke with an operator. After a few minutes, I got the full story:

"Okay Mr. Fisher, I see your account here, what's the problem?"

"The problem? The problem is there should be money in the account!"

"Calm down Mr. Fisher. I am sure there is an explanation for all this. I'm opening up your recent transactions now. I see the last transaction was made last month. It was a transfer to another bank account for about $300,000. Did you authorize a transaction?"

"No I didn't authorize that transaction! I wasn't even in the country at the time!"

"Sir, please calm down, I am sure we will be able to figure this all out."

"Figure what out! How you stole money from me?"

"Sir, I am here to assist you, if you keep yelling at me I will not be able to help you resolve this issue."

"Issue? This is my life!"

"Do you know the person that the money was transferred to? The name is Robert Fisher, is it a family member?"

"Yes," I said recognizing the name well. "It is my father."

"And does anybody else have access to this account?"

I thought for a second. The phone slid out of my sweaty palm to the carpeted floor. I could hear the woman asking if I was still there.

I stared ahead for a second, at the advertisement on the board in front of me. It was a J. Crew billboard and there was a family having a picnic. I thought of my youth and my mother buying my father and I matching Polo shirts to wear. I thought of my mother. I picked the phone up off the airport floor.

"Mr. Fisher? Are you there?

"Yes I'm here; my mother has access to my bank accounts. I signed a power of attorney over to her years ago while I was traveling abroad. Can you check if that's who transferred the funds?"

"Sure, just give me a minute to pull that information up."

I already knew the answer.

"Is your mother, Sarah Fisher?"

"Yes."

"It seems that she transferred the money out of the account."

I was silent.

"Mr. Fisher? Mr. Fisher? Are you there?"

"Yes, I am here."

The Bank Representative clicked away at her computer. I pictured her somewhere in the Philippines in her cubicle. In some ways, the banks were using the poor people of the world in the same ways I was.

"Is there anything else I can help you with today?"

"No, that's it thank you."

"Thank you for choosing Bank of America, have a—"

I hung up before she could finish her sentence. I try to call my parents, but to no surprise, they do not answer. I made my way back to the TGI Fridays, and ordered a glass of Jameson. The blonde I had been scoping before placed the drink in front of me. She smiled at me, and looked at my bags.

"Where are you flying to today?"

I took a large gulp of the Jameson, and stared into the glass after I had emptied it.

"Nowhere."

The bartender looked confused.

"So you just flew in?"

"Yeah."

"You from Miami?"

I switched between looking at her, my empty glass, and the J. Crew advertisement of the happy family.

"Yeah. No. Sort of. . ."

I got the bill, rented a car for the second time that day, and drove the two hours to my parent's house on way too much speed and Jameson to be under the legal limit.

Chapter Fifteen

Somehow, I made it to my parent's home alive. I pulled into the gated neighborhood, the rent-a-cop at the gate was new, and asked me for my ID. The neighborhood was still the same, nothing ever changed. It was as if the gate protected the families living there from things like the recession, and the burst of the high-tech bubble. The neighborhood was old money, and today's problems wouldn't affect these people. Just like the neighborhood, my mother hadn't changed much. I parked the car, and rang the doorbell. A few seconds later, my mother opened the door. She was surprised to see me. After a few moments, she got a hold of herself and the situation.

She spoke calmly at first, "What are you doing here?"

"I was in Miami, and thought I could stop by to see you. May I come in?"

"Have you quit that mess yet?"

"Not yet, that's one of the things I wanted to speak to you about."

"What's there to speak about? Quit it, sell it, do whatever you have to do, come back, re-enroll at a university, any university! And then we can speak."

She tried to shut the door, but I put my foot in the way. She continued to try to close the door on my foot. I was yelling at her now, not in anger, but in pain from my foot being crushed, and because I knew I had only a few moments to change her mind before she would shut the door on me.

"Why did you take my inheritance money? How do you expect me to quit now when I don't have any money because of you!"

"That money was for you to go to college and start a life, or to buy a house! Not for you to waste! Your grandmother didn't want it to go to this shit you're doing!"

"I'm not going to waste it! I haven't spent a single penny of the inheritance money!"

My mother quit trying to shut the door, and opened it, returning to her calmer manner. "So then why are you asking about it?"

"I want to know. That was *my* money. Grandma wanted *me* to have—"

"Don't you dare tell me what she wanted! I know what she wanted, and it wasn't this shit you're doing with your life now!"

By now the noise had gathered the attention of some neighbors who wandered nearby to see what was happening in this almost always quiet purgatory of millionaires. She changed her tone and spoke quietly.

"I took that money away for your own good. The passions of youth have obviously triumphed over your judgment, and I do not want you wasting your money. When you are a little older, and you've gotten yourself back on track, I will be more than happy to give you every single cent of the inheritance," Her voice rose in fury, "but, until then I want nothing to do with you! Now get off my property!"

The woman could change her mood quicker than a Colombian girl could get undressed.

"I'm not going anywhere. I want to work this out with you!"

I heard two doors shut one after the other, and the crowd that had been watching us went silent. We both turned away from the argument to see that two police officers had shown up at the house.

One of the police officers shined his flashlight at my eyes. I covered them to avoid the temporary blindness the act was supposed to produce. The officers separated my mother and me. One officer spoke to my mother, and the other to me. I tried to keep calm with the officer. I had never had much respect for law enforcement, and this time was no different. I could feel my anger swelling up, but I tried to be diplomatic. I ran through the basics, that my mother had taken money out of my account that I had given her power of attorney years ago. The officer scribbled little notes in the pad he had with him.

After telling my story, he looked at me and asked, "Benjamin, how much have you had to drink tonight?"

I was startled by this change of questions. Inside my chest, I felt the same deep sinking feeling I felt while leaving Medellin. Inside I realized, tonight, I might be going to jail.

"A few drinks, but I'm fine."

The officer looked unconvinced.

"Stay here, and sit your butt on the front of my squad car. I'll be back in a few minutes."

The police officer went to speak with my mother and the second officer. They spoke, often glancing over in my direction. Finally, one of the officers gave his card to my mother. She took it, and took one last look at me, before walking inside the house.

The crowd was still in front of the house, silent, and watching the most exciting event that had taken place in the neighborhood since the shenanigans of my teenage days. The silence of the crowd amplified the sound of my mother closing the front door. The two officers walked back to me.

"Benjamin, go ahead and turn around for me." Said one of the officers.

I turned around.

One of the officers put his hands over my wrists, and I could hear the clink of the handcuffs being taken out.

"You are under arrest, anything you say can and will be used against you in the court of law…"

The officer's voice trailed off, I couldn't hear the end. My life trailed off. I could not see its end. The officers helped me make my way into the backseat of the car, but I fought. *This cannot end like this*. I looked back to the front door of what used to be my home. I struggled a little with the cops and forced my way back out of the car.

"Wait, wait, what am I being arrested for? What did I do?"

"Well, first of all, trespassing."

"Trespassing? I live here, look at my ID!"

"Your mother said you haven't lived here in over a year. We spoke to a witness who said she heard your mother asking you to leave, but you didn't, and I am pretty sure by the smell of your breath, that once we take your blood at the jail you'll be going for DUI as well."

"Guys, cut me a break. All I was trying to do today is resolve some issues with my mother. I didn't hurt anybody!"

The officers were finished listening to me. They tried to force me into the backseat, and to jail. I fought them, and looked back at my front door. I head butted one of the officers. His blood splattered on my face, and I watched him hold his hand to where his nose had justbeen. I felt a nightstick hit me in the back of the head, and I fell to the ground. I knew I was being kicked, hit with a nightstick, or maced, but it didn't matter. I curled into a ball, and couldn't feel anything. I looked up to see about a dozen police.

I closed my eyes.

I woke up to a rush of hot, moist air. We had arrived to the police station, and the change in temperature from the air conditioning of the police car to the Miami heat was enough to wake me up. It would be the last sleep I would get for a long time.

The cops led me into the station and stuck me in an empty cell. I remember thinking to myself, *"This isn't so bad,"* The place was fairly clean. I sat down on the bench and began to examine my bruises. Only one of the police officers was with me now, I assume the other, with the busted nose, went to the hospital. He began to ask questions about myself to put into his report. Another officer entered with a drunken Mexican, whom he stuck in the adjoining cell. After this, another officer entered, who turned out to be a friend from high school. He sat with me through the bars, and I told him the short story of why I was sitting there in the cell that night. He laughed. I did not.

"Damn Ben, porn? Colombia? You're one crazy dude man. I gotta get back out there. Here's my card, let me know what's going on with you when you can." I took the card, and went back to re-examining my bruises. But, the work was extensive, and before I could get through half of it, the remaining arresting officer called my name and told me he was going to transport me to the jail now. I turned around, and stuck my hands through the bars and allowed him to recuff me. I never thought I would be so eager to go to jail, but every minute quicker I got booked, would mean one less minute I would have to spend in there until I posted bail.

Before he opened the cell, he asked me if I was going to behave this time, in a tone usually reserved for an animal.

The ride to jail seemed to take an eternity. I began to question the officer about the process and what would happen to me next. He explained that he was transferring me to the Miami Dade County Jail, and that there was a closer jail, but the other officer, my friend from high school, had stood up for me, and said that I was usually a stand-up guy. So, he was taking me to another jail that he thought would have less people in it, and I could get bonded out faster. I began to hate myself.

For those of you who have never seen the Miami Dade County Jail, it is a frightening edifice. The building is a ten story solid concrete creature, with one tinted window per floor. We pulled up to the inmate intake where a large steel gate adorned with barbwire on top opened up for us. When we entered the parking area I saw other police cars from all over the Miami area, some with names of neighborhoods I would never dare enter, and a large white and green bus with sirens and the word CORRECTIONS on the side of it. The system is so fucked up I would soon find out, there is nothing correct about it.

The officer parked and opened the car door for me. The dawn air was refreshing and I enjoyed my last gasps. The officer told me to stand against the wall as he walked up to the woman behind the bulletproof glass. He handed her what I assumed were the papers relating to my arrest and his gun. While this took place the bus began to unload, and a dozen men in orange jumpsuits filed out. They were escorted into the jail by three guards wearing green uniforms with the word CORRECTIONS written on their backs. The men were handcuffed and shackled by the feet to one another. Each one of them stared at me as they passed on their way to enter the jail. Every single one of them was bigger than me, and not a single one of them was white.

"I am actually going to jail," I said to myself. After the dozen or so prisoners had walked by me and looked me up and down like a piece of meat, the officer escorted me in to the jail. Entering the jail was a shock of its own. People were yelling and screaming. The change from the darkness and silence of the night air, to the lights and sounds of an overcrowded jail were overwhelming. Inside this building was like a city of its own, where there was no such thing as day and night, no windows, no hope, no privacy, no safety, no dignity, and worst of all, no freedom.

For the first time since seeing a police officer earlier today outside my parent's gated community, I was happy to have them. The officer stood in line with me to begin the intake process. Under different circumstances, this spectacle would have been quite humorous. There was a line of about 20 criminals, most of them drunk, or beaten up, being held up by their respective arresting officer. It looked like a fucked up dance line. After the bright lights, the smell of urine was the second thing to hit me. It was strong, and it was everywhere. I waited for about a half hour until it was my turn to deposit all my personal items with the guard behind the bulletproof counter. I handed over my things, and the officer signed off on everything. I was handed off from my arresting officer to one of the green uniformed jail guards, who walked me through a corridor to a row of cells. It was impossible to separate where one ended and another began from the dangle of feet, arms, and heads poking through the bars.

"Open cell three!"

A door opened. I stepped inside the cell, and looked at my new surroundings, while I faced away from the officer who took off my cuffs. The cell was packed, it seemed stuffed from floor to ceiling with bodies. Some were passed out on the floor in pools of blood and other bodily fluids. I wasn't sure if they were even alive. The floor was barely visible through the layers of crud that had amounted. There was a toilet in the corner with nothing for privacy, or for the smell. There were long rows of benches that were attached to the concrete wall. I looked to my left. The entire side of the cell was filled with black inmates. To my right, the long row of seats was occupied by Hispanic inmates. In the middle there was me. The speed and alcohol began to wear off as I heard the cell door slam shut behind me.

I stood, and was beyond the point of exhaustion, but I stood, because I didn't have any choice. There was no room on either of the rows of chairs and benches, and most of the floor was taken up by people, blood, and feces. I began to wait for whatever came next, but nothing did, except for more inmates. Soon I could no longer stand comfortably. The room was packed. I tried to take up as little space as possible. I tried to disappear. But, not only could I not disappear, I couldn't breathe. The 30 or so other people in the room seemed to have sucked the place dry of all available oxygen. I lost track of time.

Finally, a guard called my name. Cell number three opened up again, I wondered how many times it had opened and closed in its lifetime. I was told to undress on top of a folded cardboard box. I do, and am told to bend over and cough. I wondered if this was how my girls felt when they met me for the first time. After this, I redressed, and got my photos and fingerprints taken. Finally, I made my way to wait in line and make the notorious first phone call inmates are allowed after being arrested. I stood and waited. I watched the older six foot six black man with grey hair in front of me make his phone call to, judging by his tone of voice, his mother, or grandmother. I closed my eyes and pictured a small, frail, women on the other end of the phone call. In a small apartment with a cross on the wall, she sadly rejected to offer to pay his bail, and I wondered how many times before this night, he had asked her for bail. I watched him hang up the phone; his large frame was unable to hide his disappointment. I walked to the phone, and was unable to figure out how to dial. One of the guards came over and helped me. I dialed Alejandro's number, the phone rang, and I heard him pick up.

"Hel—"

"Alejandro, its Ben, I'm in Miami Dade County Jail bail me out as soon as you can!"

"Who is this?"

"It's Ben! You're fucking partner! I'm in jail! I need you to bail me out!"

Alejandro was surprised; he thought I was back in Medellin until now.

"Alright, I'm on it. I'm on my way."

I hung up the phone, and made my way with the guard upstairs. I thought of the possibility of Alejandro getting me out of there, and being out of that fucking cell finally! A smile almost crept onto my face, until I looked at the sign next to the row of cells we were about to enter. It read first in English, then under it in Spanish, and below that in Creole:

IF YOU ARE RAPED OR SEXUALLY ASSAULTED, PLEASE CONTACT A CORRECTIONS OFFICER IMMEDIATELY.

Before the message could register, I had been shoved into a new room. The door slammed shut behind me. In front of me were three black men with dread locks sitting on a picnic bench chained to the floor, watching a football game being shown on the television outside the bars of the cell. I looked around and counted 20 bunk beds, 40 beds, and 55 people. On the floor, I saw a rat go by.

Opposite the bunk beds were three pay phones cemented into the wall. Some inmates stared at me, and others went about their business. I was the only one not in an orange jumpsuit at this point. Besides being white, my green Polo shorts, white dress shirt, and Marc Jacobs flip-flops didn't fool anyone into thinking I was Al Capone. I started to think about the sign I had read just before entering this cage. I walked immediately toward the phones, trying to dial, but I couldn't get it to work. The message explained the directions to me in Creole. While this was going on, I noticed a group of about five Hispanic men sitting in the left corner bunk beds diagonal from me, staring at me, and speaking with one another. I continued to try to dial Alejandro. Two of the guys began to move closer to me, walking around me, and sizing me up. I wanted to cry. I wanted my mother's love. I wanted freedom. I wanted safety. But, I didn't let these people see any of that; I just kept trying to read the phone directions on the wall, and dial. Finally, one of the men who had been circling near me said something to me.

"Yo man!"

"Yeah?"

He looked me up and down again. I prepared my hands for a fight, my exhausted body pumped blood faster in anticipation.

"You need some help dialing?"

"Umm… Yeah man, please."

I gave him the number and he dialed for me. He explained to me that before dialing I had to put in my jail ID number so they could track our phone calls. I put in the number that was now my new identity and finally heard Alejandro's familiar voice on the other end. He told me not to worry and that he was on his way with bail money. He already knew the details of my case, through the Miami Police website, and had already contacted a lawyer for me. I hung up. The inmate who had helped me dial was still there when I returned from my little break from reality.

"So what? Is you a lawyer or some shit?"

"Something like that."

"So what you in here for man?"

"I hit a cop."

The inmate didn't know whether to believe me or not, "You got your arrest sheet Papo? Let me see it."

He didn't wait for an answer, and grabbed the orange slip of paper out of my hands. He began to read it, a smile came across his face the longer he stared at it.

"Yo! You wasn't playing; it says you broke the fuckin' cop's nose! You's one crazy ass white boy! Come chill with us first timer!"

I followed him back to the corner he and his crew were occupying. I was introduced to the guys and shook hands with all of them. I soon found out that the guy who helped me dial was named Pepe, here for possession and intent to sell Cocaine. One of the other guys, a darker fellow with a blowout, named Pablo, as the tattoo across his neck displayed, asked me, "So what you in here for man?"

"It's a long story."

"Shit Nigga, we in jail, we aint got nothing but time."

Everyone laughed a little, even me.

I told Pablo about Colombia, the business, my family the arrest. The others in the crew became interested in the story as well. They asked me all sorts of questions about the girls, about traveling, what countries I had been to, how different it was than America? Soon the crew was sitting on the floor opposite me, one of them had temporarily given up their bed for me to sit and talk. I felt how a parent must feel when they come into their kid's school to explain to their class about their job for career day. They all told me not to worry, that with a first offense, I probably wouldn't even get probation with the right lawyer working for me. But their words weren't enough. I felt the deep sinking feeling again that I had experienced periodically since the beginning of this trip to Miami. What I was provoked by even surprised me. What scared me most about being arrested was the record. I wondered if I still would be able to go back to college as my family had always planned for me.

Throughout the day, the guys kept introducing me to other prisoners in the cell. One man in his 40's or 50's told me not to worry, that he was facing 70 years, and he was already 55—he was going to die in there. He explained to me that he was awaiting transport to a federal facility for gun trafficking. His cheeriness and his acceptance of fate scared everything I had left right out of me. Another inmate tried to comfort me telling me how he hadn't seen his baby girl being born, and to remember him when I got out in a few hours. I took in all the stories. I stood in one of the corners, away from all the people and stories I had just heard—and I cried. With the endorsement of Pablo and his boys, I finally felt safe enough to let out everything I had been holding in since telling my mother about my porn business over a year ago. Pablo and another one of the crew came over. Pablo put a hand on my shoulder.

"I know Papi; you're going to get through this man.

We're going to get through this."

I cried deeper, it spread, and soon Pablo was crying too.

"We're going to get out of this shit don't you worry Papi!"

I went back to our corner and laid down for a little.

The air conditioning was on so cold it was impossible to sleep. The guys talked about their own convictions, possible time, possibilities of bail, and the future; any subject to pass the hours. Here are some of their comments:

One of the guys looked at me. "Man, once I get out of here, I'm never coming back to jail! I'm going back for my GED, find myself a 9-5 job, I might not ever get rich, but it's better than being in here."

"That's great man, you're right." I said.

"I'm gonna get out of here, sell the rest of the brick I got stored, and with that money I'll be straight for a fresh start."

I heard more stories, heard of girls past, hookers, robberies; a fight broke out over somebody taking someone else's bed sheets. One of the guys in the bunk bed next to me had sickle cell. The other guys did their best to help him through his attack. Even in jail, I witnessed people helping one another for no other reason than it was the right thing to do.

28 hours after arriving to the planet known as Miami Dade County Jail, my bail was posted. The door to our cell opened and my name was called. People shook my hand, and we told each other good luck and other farewells. Pablo asked me to call his girlfriend for him, just to tell her he's okay and that he loved her. The door shut before he could shout the last two digits of her phone number.

Chapter Sixteen

Alejandro and Estaban waited outside the jail for me. I got out, picked up my property through the window, and we made our way to Estaban's car. We got in and we were all silent.

"Dude, you stink like shit." Said Estaban.

"Just drive the fucking car."

"Where to?"

"Take me to the *Diplomat Hotel*; I need a long shower, and a big bed."

As we drove off to the hotel, I told them what had the events of the day since our meeting at the strip club; the airport, driving drunk, head butting the cop, and what jail was like. They stayed silent and listened to me for the entire time. We arrived at the *Diplomat*, and I booked a room. Alejandro and Estaban asked if I wanted them to stay. I told them yes, that I needed to go to our office afterward. I showered for what felt like an eternity, and put the water so hot that it burned my skin. No matter how many times I scrubbed myself with soap, I still didn't feel clean. Over an hour later, I emerged from the bathroom. Alejandro had brought some spare clothes for me. I dressed and we left for the office.

In the office, I grabbed a briefcase I had hidden in one of the file cabinets. Alejandro left me back at the hotel. I told him that I was going to rest and would speak to him the next day. I took the briefcase upstairs, showered again, and got into a bathrobe before opening the briefcase. There was only one thing in it, a pistol. I ordered a bottle of Jameson up to my room, and examined the gun. I contemplated ending my own life. I looked at the pistol, how clean the stainless steel was, almost sterile. It's funny, when I think of death, I think of the table of morgues, and the stainless steel of weapons. In a way, death seems lot cleaner than life. My whiskey arrived. I had a few glasses, and a few more glances at the gun, but I didn't have the energy or the want to commit suicide. I fell into a deep sleep. When I woke up 16 hours later, I again returned to the shower. I ordered room service and ate for the first time in over two days. After that, I ordered a cab back to our office. I put the briefcase back into its hiding spot for another time I hoped would never arrive.

Since I was out on bail, and technically was never asked to stay within the country, I took my chances and headed back to Colombia. After all, we had studios to fill. I also had another reason for going back besides strictly monetary. I wanted to remember the adventure and potential success that I really believed in when I had started this business. I wanted to try to understand what had once brought me so much fulfillment and excitement, and what brought others so much suspicion and distrust and what had begun to change my feelings for my girlfriend. I still think I was the same. Maybe I wasn't. Maybe it had changed me. When I would come back to Miami for vacations, people said that I no longer cared for other people. Gone were the days of socializing with new people all the time. I didn't care about what anybody else was doing, just about my partners, my employees, and me. Employees that I really didn't even know anymore, employees that I never really knew. I thought to myself. That morning after a hot bath at the *Diplomat*, I used my Canadian passport to fly to Medellin.

I remember, of course, the airport.

I had been stranded at the Bogota airport for two hours awaiting my connecting flight. Another time I would have stayed for a couple of days, but these were not festive times. I kept looking at my Colombian cell phone waiting for Alejandro to say that the police had been by the office looking for me. But, no call came. One hour, one Xanax, and one glass of Jameson and I was back in what had begun to feel like my second home, Medellin, surrounded in the warm embrace of friends. Andres had come to greet me, as well as Erica. Ruben, D-Money, and three women I had never seen before came as well. Andres introduced them as, Anna, Martina, and Claudia.

"These are some of your newest employees."

Martina smiled and said, "It's an honor to meet you Jefe."

I took another Xanax.

"Alright let's hit it."

We drove away from the airport, and into Medellin. Andres passed a blunt back to me, and I have déjà vu of simpler times, happier times. The radio played Jay-Z and Lil Wayne's *Mr. Carter*, Andres and Ruben changed the lyrics to *Mr. Fisher*.

"Hey Mr. Fisher, where you been? I been hustling... Around the globe now I'm back again."

My shoulders laid back into the seat of the Mercedes I had gotten to know so well. It's the first moment I can remember that I had been able to relax since my arrest.

"Where we headed?" I asked.

Andres looked at me. "I was thinking we could head out to Circus, celebrate your return."

"These aren't celebratory times my friend, I'm facing the possibility of 15 years in prison, I head butted a Miami cop."

"You head-butted a cop?"

Neither of us said anything.

"Somebody must have really pissed you off to do somethin' that fuckin' stupid!"

Andres cracked out laughing. He raised his hand in apology and composed himself.

"Parce, everything's going to be good man. Listen, you're white, I know you got some good ass lawyer you can call, some uncle or some shit. It's your first offence?"

"Yeah."

"Don't sweat it man you're good."

"Well that's only part of the problem, but fuck it, I don't wanna talk about it."

One of our newest employees broke in, "Padonde vamos?" They looked at Andres, who looked at me. I told them I wanted to stop by one of the studios, and take a look at how things were running.

Andres reached for his phone to let them know of our arrival. I stopped him.

"No, no, don't tell them we're coming."

Andres maneuvered left, at the red light there were four black man piled upon one another's shoulder reaching into the sky, begging for money. Our Mercedes brought attention to us. This could be a very dangerous thing in parts of the city. Two different vendors approached the car, one attempted to clean the windshield. Andres honked at him and lurched the car forward. The vendor retreated. The second appeared on the passenger side, where Ruben was sitting, after telling the vendor that he wasn't interested, Ruben got upset, opened the window and pushed the vendor on the pavement, breaking all of his merchandise in the process. Ruben shut the door to the car, and muttered in Spanish something about "these cockroaches from the mountains." The Xanax and whiskey and the possibility of incarceration can quickly change the views of even the brightest idealists. I let the incident pass. A year ago, I would have yelled at Ruben, and given the vendor money for the broken merchandise. Now I realized that I could never change, nor understand, everything about this mystic land and the beautiful, insane, people who inhabit it.

127

We arrived at the Las Brujas studio. Everything was like I had left it. It was only my life that had changed completely in the past 72 hours. I went to my office in back and poured myself a glass of whiskey. The three girls who had come with Andres and Ruben to greet me at the airport joined me in the room. One of them began to undress and the other two made their way over to me, and began to kiss my neck, and lick my ears.

Martina whispered, "Do you want to see how well your girls can satisfy a client?"

I pushed the girls away. I thanked the three of them, and told them I would take a rain check, and sent them back to work. I went back to my glass of Jameson and my world of thoughts.

Chapter Seventeen

I wound up moving in permanently to my old room at the Pit Stop Hostel, the *Pussy Pink*. I started to spend a lot of time with my employees outside of the studios, just seeing their everyday lives, hearing their stories, how much the money and benefits from the job had improved both their lives and their children's lives. The next few weeks I was a ghost at the studios when I wasn't with one of my employees, I would be doing something like buying toys and giving it out to kids in the slums, or helping out at a local food drive. After this, I still had no answer about my future plans, no answers about anything really. I spent a couple of days just riding the subways, looking at the city, watching the everyday working people go about their lives, writing bad poetry, drinking Jameson in a bag, writing bad poetry, drinking Jameson in a bag. I was lost. When I was in Medellin, I was a different person—my alter ego. Here, I actually felt like I was making a difference, my family, my court dates ahead, and spending my money from what I had built here on a defense attorney, instead of towards our website, made Medellin all the more alluring.

.

End

In the end, there was no moment of clarity like they always describe in movies and books. I never found an answer to whether I should leave or not. It didn't end like that. The city of Miami dropped the charges against me shortly after I arrived back in the United States. We spent the next few months working our asses off, eventually setting up four new studios, giving us a total of seven studios, approximately 140 employees working at any particular hour of any particular day. At the same time, Estaban, Alejandro and I began to save up money for our own website. We took in Andres and Ruben as partners too. They began to sacrifice their salaries to contribute.

Exactly two years, three months, and fourteen days after stepping foot in Colombia we had built our own website. The last few days before switching over to our website were more hectic then anything we had experienced up until that point. All the employees during their last shifts sent out messages to all fan club members that they would be switching to a new site. This had to be done efficiently and coordinated, because as soon as the website we were working for figured out that we were trying to steal their clients, all of our accounts would be blocked from the site. The investment turned out to be quite lucrative for us. Now that Ruben and Andres were partners, we didn't need somebody else there twenty-four hours a day. And I had begun to find myself in a lot of airports besides just that of Medellin, Bogota, and Miami. I started to invest my money in different opportunities outside of porno, specifically real estate in Miami. When I saw what we were discussing didn't make any sense to me, I decided to enroll in a few business courses at school. That's how it went. My life eventually began to refocus to Miami. First from investments, then school and trips to Medellin began to decrease from once every two weeks, to once a month, to once every two months. Two years after the launch of our website, and six months before receiving my Bachelor's degree in Business, I sold my portion of the company to some of the partners in exchange for a large check, and a contract guaranteeing me a certain percentage of the profit for a certain allotted amount of time. Ruben drove me in his Mercedes one last time to the airport, this time he was no longer my employee, just one of my closest friends. I made my way inside and through security. I sat down in the same waiting area where this journey and this book began. I stretched, and smiled. I made my way over to the large window, and watched a plane that was circling to land. I thought of its passengers; who they were, and what they were doing. Somebody was coming home, somebody was leaving home, and somebody was beginning an adventure. One story begins, and one story ends.

Acknowledgements

No one writes a book without help. First, I want to thank God for giving me this story to tell and the abilities to tell it. I would also like to thank my family.

In this long process, I have others who helped me along the way. I would like to thank my editor and literary advisor, Jody Mabry. In addition, I thank Dicky Phillips, for his editorial help, as well as Gabrielle Liedtke and Lisa Brennan for illustration.

Lastly, among the list of many, there are Alex Phillips, Leah Taylor, Shyne Po, Levi Meyers, Ariel Pellegrino, Joshua Needle, Chucky Samuels, Yehuda Fishman, Ryan Nixon, Ladawon Lubertine, and all the people that inspired the characters of this book.

Finally, to the City and People of Medellin, thank you.